GRADES K-2

...the Super Source™
Snap™ Cubes

Cuisenaire Company of America, Inc.
White Plains, NY

Cuisenaire extends its warmest thanks to the many teachers and students across the country who helped ensure the success of the Super Source™ series by participating in the outlining, writing, and field testing of the materials.

Project Director: Judith Adams
Managing Editor: Doris Hirschhorn
Editorial Team: John Nelson, Deborah J. Slade, Harriet Slonim
Field Test Coordinator: Laurie Verdeschi

Design Manager: Phyllis Aycock
Text Design: Amy Berger, Tracey Munz
Line Art and Production: Joan Lee, Fiona Santoianni
Cover Design: Michael Muldoon
Illustrations: Rebecca Thornburgh

the Super Source™
Table of Contents

Using the Super Source™

The Super Source™ is a series of books each of which contains a collection of activities to use with a specific math manipulative. Driving the Super Source™ is Cuisenaire's conviction that children construct their own understandings through rich, hands-on mathematical experiences. Although the activities in each book are written for a specific grade range, they all connect to the core of mathematics learning that is important to every K-6 child. Thus, the material in many activities can easily be refocused for children at other grade levels. Because the activities are not arranged sequentially, children can work on any activity at any time.

The lessons in the Super Source™ all follow a basic structure consistent with the vision of mathematics teaching described in the Curriculum and Evaluation Standards for School Mathematics published by the National Council of Teachers of Mathematics.

All of the activities in this series involve Problem Solving, Communication, Reasoning, and Mathematical Connections—the first four NCTM Standards. Each activity also focuses on one or more of the following curriculum strands: Number, Geometry, Measurement, Patterns/Functions, Probability/Statistics, Logic.

HOW LESSONS ARE ORGANIZED

At the beginning of each lesson, you will find, to the right of the title, both the major curriculum strands to which the lesson relates and the particular topics that children will work with. Each lesson has three main sections. The first, GETTING READY, offers an Overview, which states what children will be doing, and why, and a list of "What You'll Need." Specific numbers of Snap Cubes are suggested on this list but can be adjusted as the needs of your specific situation dictate. Before an activity, cubes can be counted out and placed in containers of self-sealing plastic bags for easy distribution. If appropriate for an activity, the cubes might be distributed as color rods, 10 cubes per color. When crayons are called for, it is understood that their colors are those that match the Snap Cubes and that markers may be used in place of crayons. Blackline masters that are provided for your convenience at the back of the book are referenced on this list. Paper, pencils, scissors, tape, and materials for making charts, which are necessary in certain activities, are usually not.

Although overhead Snap Cubes are always listed in "What You'll Need" as optional, these materials are highly effective when you want to demonstrate the use of Snap Cubes. As you move the cubes on the screen, children can work with the same materials at their seats. Children can also use the overhead to present their work to other members of their group or to the class.

The second section, THE ACTIVITY, first presents a possible scenario for Introducing the children to the activity. The aim of this brief introduction is to help you give children the tools they will need to investigate independently. However, care has been taken to avoid undercutting the activity itself. Since these investigations are designed to enable children to increase their own mathematical power, the idea is to set the stage but not steal the show! The heart of the lesson, On Their Own, is found in a box at the top of the second page of each lesson. Here, rich problems stimulate many different problem-solving approaches and lead to a variety of solutions. These hands-on explorations have the potential for bringing children to new mathematical ideas and deepening skills.

On Their Own is intended as a stand-alone activity for children to explore with a partner or in a small group. Be sure to make the needed directions clearly visible. You may want to write them on the chalkboard or on an overhead or present them either on reusable cards or paper. For children who may have difficulty reading the directions, you can read them aloud or make sure that at least one "reader" is in each group.

The last part of this second section, *The Bigger Picture*, gives suggestions for how children can share their work and their thinking and make mathematical connections. Class charts and children's recorded work provide a springboard for discussion. Under "Thinking and Sharing," there are several prompts that you can use to promote discussion. Children will not be able to respond to these prompts with one-word answers. Instead, the prompts encourage children to describe what they notice, tell how they found their results, and give the reasoning behind their answers. Thus children learn to verify their own results rather than relying on the teacher to determine if an answer is "right" or "wrong." Though the class discussion might immediately follow the investigation, it is important not to cut the activity short by having a class discussion too soon.

The Bigger Picture often includes a suggestion for a "Writing" (or drawing) assignment. This is meant to help children process what they have just been doing. You might want to use these ideas as a focus for daily or weekly entries in a math journal that each child keeps.

From: *Two-Color Patterns*

From: *Ten Towers of Ten*

The Bigger Picture always ends with ideas for "Extending the Activity." Extensions take the essence of the main activity and either alter or extend its parameters. These activities are well used with a class that becomes deeply involved in the primary activity or for children who finish before the others. In any case, it is probably a good idea to expose the entire class to the possibility of, and the results from, such extensions.

The third and final section of the lesson is TEACHER TALK. Here, in *Where's the Mathematics?*, you can gain insight into the underlying mathematics of the activity and discover some of the strategies children are apt to use as they work. Solutions are also given—when such are necessary and/or helpful. Because *Where's the Mathematics?* provides a view of what may happen in the lesson as well as the underlying mathematical potential that may grow out of it, this may be the section that you want to read before presenting the activity to children.

USING THE ACTIVITIES

The Super Source™ has been designed to fit into the variety of classroom environments in which it will be used. These range from a completely manipulative-based classroom to one in which manipulatives are just beginning to play a part. You may choose to use some activities in *the Super Source*™ in the way set forth in each lesson (introducing an activity to the whole class, then breaking the class up into groups that all work on the same task, and so forth). You will then be able to circulate among the groups as they work to observe and perhaps comment on each child's work. This approach requires a full classroom set of materials but allows you to concentrate on the variety of ways that children respond to a given activity.

Alternatively, you may wish to make two or three related activities available to different groups of children at the same time. You may even wish to use different manipulatives to explore the same mathematical concept. (Cuisenaire® Rods and Color Tiles, for example, can be used to teach some of the same concepts as Snap Cubes.) This approach does not require full classroom sets of a particular manipulative. It also permits greater adaptation of materials to individual children's needs and/or preferences.

If children are comfortable working independently, you might want to set up a "menu"— that is, set out a number of related activities from which children can choose. Children should be encouraged to write about their experiences with these independent activities.

However you choose to use *the Super Source*™ activities, it would be wise to allow time for several groups or the entire class to share their experiences. The dynamics of this type of interaction, in which children share not only solutions and strategies but also feelings and intuitions, is the basis of continued mathematical growth. It allows children who are beginning to form a mathematical structure to clarify it and those who have mastered just isolated concepts to begin to see how these concepts might fit together.

Again, both the individual teaching style and combined learning styles of the children should dictate the specific method of utilizing *the Super Source*™ lessons. At first sight, some activities may appear too difficult for some of your children, and you may find yourself tempted to actually "teach" by modeling exactly how an activity can lead to a particular learning outcome. If you do this, you rob children of the chance to try the activity in whatever way they can. As long as children have a way to begin an investigation, give them time and opportunity to see it through. Instead of making assumptions about what children will or won't do, watch and listen. The excitement and challenge of the activity—as well as the chance to work cooperatively—may bring out abilities in children that will surprise you.

If you are convinced, however, that an activity does not suit your students, adjust it, by all means. You may want to change the language, either by simplifying it or by referring to specific vocabulary that you and your children already use and are comfortable with. On the other hand, if you suspect that an activity isn't challenging enough, you may want to read through the activity extensions for a variation that you can give children instead.

RECORDING

Although the direct process of working with Snap Cubes is a valuable one, it is afterward, when children look at, compare, share, and think about their constructions, that an activity yields its greatest rewards. However, because Snap Cube designs can't always be left intact, children need an effective way to record their work. To this end, at the back of this book recording paper is provided for reproduction. The "What You'll Need" listing at the beginning of each lesson often specifies the kind of recording paper to use. For example, it seems natural for children to record Snap Cube patterns on grid paper. Yet it is important for children to use a method of recording that they feel comfortable with. Frustration in recording their structures can leave children feeling that the actual activity was either too difficult or just not fun! Thus, there may be times when you feel that children should just share their work rather than record it.

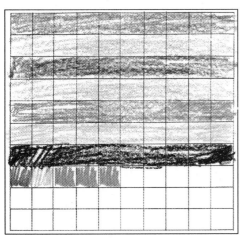

From: *Closest to 100*

From: *Two-Color Patterns*

Young children might duplicate their work on grid paper by coloring in boxes on grids that exactly match the cubes in size. Older children may be able to use smaller grids or even construct the recording paper as they see fit.

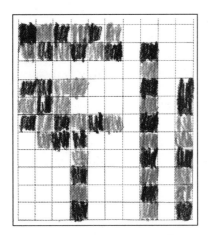

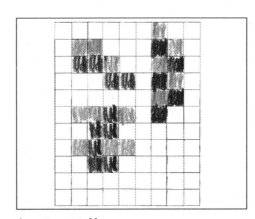

From: *Showing One Half*

An interesting way to "freeze" a Snap Cube design is to create it using a software piece, such as *Building Perspective*, and then get a printout. Children can use a classroom or resource-room computer if it is available or, where possible, extend the activity into a home assignment by utilizing their home computers.

Recording involves more than copying structures. Writing, drawing, and making charts and tables are also ways to record. By creating a table of data gathered in the course of their investigations, children are able to draw conclusions and look for patterns. When children write or draw, either in their group or later by themselves, they are clarifying their understanding of their recent mathematical experience.

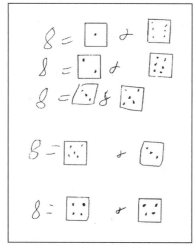

From: Some Sums

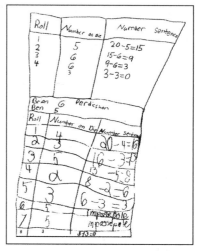

From: The Disappearing Train

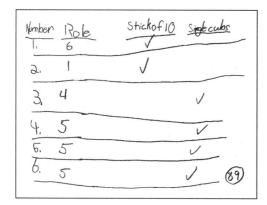

From: Closest to 100

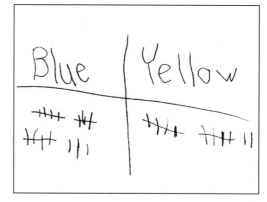

From: Sneak a Peek

With a roomful of children busily engaged in their investigations, it is not easy for a teacher to keep track of how individual children are working. Having tangible material to gather and examine when the time is right will help you to keep in close touch with each child's learning.

Exploring Snap™ Cubes

Snap Cubes are a versatile collection of three-quarter-inch interlocking cubes which come in ten colors and connect on all six sides. They are pleasant to handle, easy to manipulate and, although simple in concept, can be used to develop a wide variety of mathematical ideas at many different levels of complexity. Since Snap Cubes come in ten different colors, the cubes are useful for developing patterns, both one- and two-dimensional, based on color. The cubes can be arranged in a single layer to naturally fit into a square grid pattern, or they can be used to cover positions on a printed grid or game board. When the cubes are used to build three-dimensional structures, they lead naturally to the concepts of volume and surface area.

$$20 - 5 = 15$$
$$15 - 1 = 14$$
$$14 - 4 = 10$$
$$10 - 2 = 8$$
$$8 - 6 = 2$$
$$2 - 2 = 0$$

From: *The Disappearing Train*

The colors of the Snap Cubes can also be used to identify cubes in other contexts. For example, the different colors can represent designated quantities in various number situations. They become a sampling device when they are drawn from a bag, and they aid in concretely building bar graphs.

We rolled mostly sixes, sevens and ates.

From: *Some Sums*

WORKING WITH SNAP™ CUBES

Snap Cubes make natural and appealing counters. Since they snap together firmly, they are useful for young children as number models. If children build a stick corresponding to each number from 1 to 10, it is natural for them to arrange them in a staircase and to talk about greater and less, longer and shorter. Numbers might also be represented by the following cube patterns, which are easily sorted into "even" ones, in which each cube is paired with another, and "odd" ones, in which there is an "odd man out."

Snap Cubes also help children to more easily see relationships such as the following:

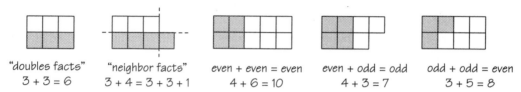

| "doubles facts" | "neighbor facts" | even + even = even | even + odd = odd | odd + odd = even |
| 3 + 3 = 6 | 3 + 4 = 3 + 3 + 1 | 4 + 6 = 10 | 4 + 3 = 7 | 3 + 5 = 8 |

Since there are large numbers of cubes in a set of Snap Cubes, they are useful for estimation and for developing number sense. Children can make a long rod with the cubes, estimate how many there are in the rod, and then separate the rod into sticks of 10, identify how many tens they have, and count the "leftovers" to find how many ones there are.

The colors of the cubes further make them useful in developing the concept of place value. Each color can represent a place value, and children can play exchange games in which, if they have 10 of one color, they can exchange them for one of the next color.

Snap Cubes are very suitable for developing understanding of the meaning of addition. They can be used as loose counters, with a different color for each addend. The colors can also broaden children's understanding of subtraction. Children often think initially of subtraction as "take away." To act out 6 – 4, children put out 6 cubes and take away 4.

Snap Cubes are also ideal for developing the concept of multiplication, both as grouping and as an array. To show 3 x 4, children can make 3 "cube trains" with 4 in each and count them all. Arranging these cubes in a rectangular array not only makes it visually easy to understand why 3 x 4 = 4 x 3 but also leads naturally into a model for understanding the formula for the area of a rectangle. In addition, Snap Cubes are suitable for exploring area, perimeter, volume, and surface area relations.

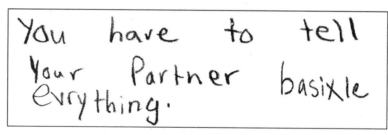

From: *Make a Copy*

Snap Cubes are a wonderful tool to use in helping children to represent numbers in terms of factors and to understand procedures of finding greatest common divisors and least common multiples. Snap Cubes are also a natural unit for length, and using them can lead to early experience of ratio and proportion. Children can measure the same length in Snap Cubes and in another unit, perhaps inches. They can record their results for a few different lengths. They may then measure in just one unit and predict the measure in the other.

ASSESSING CHILDREN'S UNDERSTANDING

Snap Cubes are wonderful tools for assessing children's mathematical thinking. Watching children work on their Snap Cubes gives you a sense of how they approach a mathematical problem. Their thinking can be "seen," in so far as that thinking is expressed through the way they construct, recognize, and continue spatial patterns. When a class breaks up into small working groups, you are able to circulate, listen, and raise questions, all the while focusing on how individuals are thinking. Here is a perfect opportunity for authentic assessment.

Having children describe their structures and share their strategies and thinking with the whole class gives you another opportunity for observational assessment. Furthermore, you may want to gather children's recorded work or invite them to choose pieces to add to their math portfolios.

My Pridiction is Lots of threes

Because it wood be better if you used a difont number.

If my Littel sister wood whant to no I wood tell her to pick 10 because it has a Lot of wase to get 10.

From: *Some Sums*

If there were three colers it would be harder to gesse. I would take alot of peres.

From: *Sneak a Peek*

Models of teachers assessing children's understanding can be found in Cuisenaire's series of videotapes listed below. Snap Cubes can be used in many of the lessons shown on the *Color Tiles* and *Six Models* tapes.

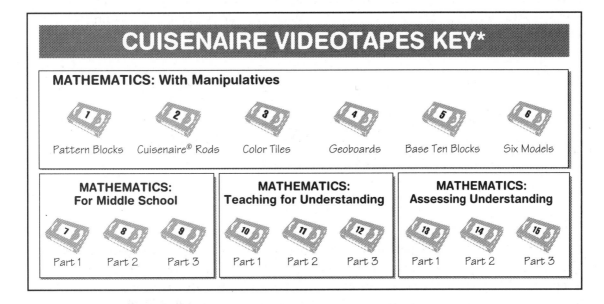

CUISENAIRE VIDEOTAPES KEY*

MATHEMATICS: With Manipulatives

| 1 Pattern Blocks | 2 Cuisenaire® Rods | 3 Color Tiles | 4 Geoboards | 5 Base Ten Blocks | 6 Six Models |

MATHEMATICS: For Middle School	**MATHEMATICS: Teaching for Understanding**	**MATHEMATICS: Assessing Understanding**
7 Part 1 8 Part 2 9 Part 3	10 Part 1 11 Part 2 12 Part 3	13 Part 1 14 Part 2 15 Part 3

STRANDS

	PROBLEM SOLVING	COMMUNICATION	REASONING	CONNECTIONS	Geometry	Logic	Measurement	Number	Patterns/Functions	Probability/Statistics
AT THE CRAYON FACTORY	◆	◆	◆	◆				◆		◆
CLOSEST TO 100	◆	◆	◆	◆				◆		
DIVIDING 24	◆	◆	◆	◆				◆		
HOW LONG IS IT?	◆	◆	◆	◆	◆	◆	◆	◆		
HOW MANY TRAINS?	◆	◆	◆	◆				◆		◆
MAKE A COPY	◆	◆	◆	◆	◆					
MIRRORED IMAGES	◆	◆	◆	◆	◆					
MULTIPLES OF 10	◆	◆	◆	◆				◆		
ON THE METER MARK	◆	◆	◆	◆			◆			◆
PUZZLES	◆	◆	◆	◆	◆		◆			
RED OR BLUE?	◆	◆	◆	◆						◆
SHOWING ONE HALF	◆	◆	◆	◆	◆			◆		
SNEAK A PEEK	◆	◆	◆	◆				◆		◆
SOME SUMS	◆	◆	◆	◆				◆		◆
TEN TOWERS OF TEN	◆	◆	◆					◆		◆
THE DISAPPEARING TRAIN	◆	◆	◆	◆				◆		◆
THE HUMAN BALANCE SCALE	◆	◆	◆	◆			◆			
TWO-COLOR PATTERNS	◆	◆	◆	◆		◆		◆	◆	

TOPICS

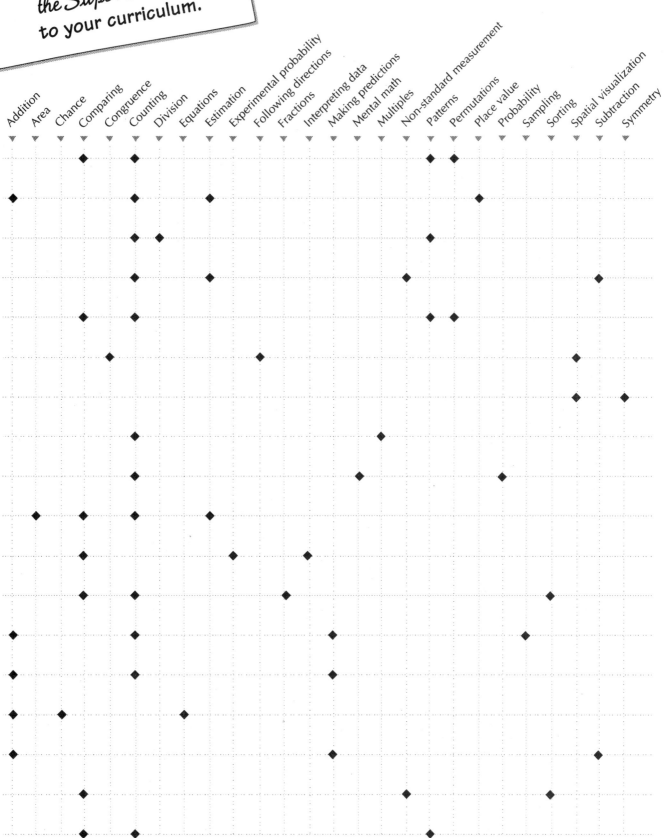

Topics (columns, left to right): Addition, Area, Chance, Comparing, Congruence, Counting, Division, Equations, Estimation, Experimental probability, Following directions, Fractions, Interpreting data, Making predictions, Mental math, Multiples, Non-standard measurement, Patterns, Permutations, Place value, Probability, Sampling, Sorting, Spatial visualization, Subtraction, Symmetry

Classroom-tested activities contained in these *Super Source*™ Snap™ Cubes books focus on the math strands in the charts below.

...the Super Source™ Snap™ Cubes, Grades 3-4

Geometry	Logic	Measurement
Number	Patterns/Functions	Probability/Statistics

...the Super Source™ Snap™ Cubes, Grades 5-6

Geometry	Logic	Measurement
Number	Patterns/Functions	Probability/Statistics

Classroom-tested activities contained in these *Super Source*™ books focus on the math strands as indicated in these charts.

the Super Source™ Tangrams, Grades K-2

Geometry	Logic	Measurement
Number	**Patterns/Functions**	**Probability/Statistics**

the Super Source™ Cuisenaire® Rods, Grades K-2

Geometry	Logic	Measurement
Number	**Patterns/Functions**	**Probability/Statistics**

the Super Source™ Geoboards, Grades K-2

Geometry	Logic	Measurement
Number	**Patterns/Functions**	**Probability/Statistics**

the Super Source™ Color Tiles, Grades K-2

Geometry	Logic	Measurement
Number	**Patterns/Functions**	**Probability/Statistics**

the Super Source™ Pattern Blocks, Grades K-2

Geometry	Logic	Measurement
Number	**Patterns/Functions**	**Probability/Statistics**

Overview of the Lessons

Snap™ Cubes, Grades K-2

AT THE CRAYON FACTORY

- • Permutations
- • Patterns
- • Comparing
- • Counting

Getting Ready

What You'll Need

100 Snap Cubes, 25 each of 4 different colors per group

The Crayon Factory recording sheets, 4 sheets per group, page 90

Overhead Snap Cubes (optional)

Overview

Children use different-colored Snap Cubes to model the colors of crayons and try to find the number of ways four different-colored crayons can be arranged in a box. In this activity, children have the opportunity to:

- ◆ discover that there are many different ways to arrange four colors
- ◆ look for patterns

The Activity

Introducing

- ◆ On the board, sketch an open crayon box with one row of three crayons. Ask children how many ways they think a crayon manufacturer could arrange a blue, a yellow, and a red crayon in the box.

- ◆ Tell children that you are going to use Snap Cubes to represent the crayons. Then connect a blue, a yellow, and a red Snap Cube to make a train that shows one possible way to arrange the crayons.

- ◆ Have children help you find other arrangements showing different ways to order the three colors. Place each new arrangement next to the ones already found.

- ◆ Establish that for three colors, there are a total of six arrangements:

blue-yellow-red	yellow-blue-red	red-blue-yellow
blue-red-yellow	yellow-red-blue	red-yellow-blue

On Their Own

> How many different ways can you arrange 4 different-colored crayons in a crayon box?
>
> - Work with a group. Choose 4 different-colored Snap Cubes to represent the colors of the crayons. You will need 4 recording sheets that look like this:
>
> - Each of you build a 4-cube train using 1 of each of the 4 colors.
>
> - Compare your train with those made by the others in your group.
>
>   - If the trains show different arrangements, set them aside.
>
>   - If any of the trains are the same, set aside only one of them.
>
> - Continue working together to make trains until you think you have found all the possible arrangements using your 4 colors.
>
> - Record your group's work by coloring in the different arrangements on the recording sheet.
>
> - See if you can figure out a way to tell whether your group found all the possible arrangements.

The Bigger Picture

Thinking and Sharing

Ask a volunteer from each group to display the group's Snap Cube trains. Depending on the colors that the various groups used, collect and arrange the trains in such a way that children can look at and compare the groups' findings.

Use prompts such as these to promote class discussion:

- How many possible arrangements of the four colors do you think there are?

- How are any two of the arrangements alike? How are they different?

- How can you arrange the Snap Cube trains so that you know you have found all of the possible ways to arrange the four crayons?

- What patterns do you see that help you determine if you have found all of the arrangements?

You may want to suggest that children sort the trains by the color of the first cube on the left, then the second cube from the left, and so on.

Drawing

Have children use the information on their recording sheets to color another recording sheet to show the arrangements of the crayons in a more organized way. For example, they could show all the arrangements that start with red, then all the arrangements that start with blue, and so on.

Extending the Activity

1. Have children find a possible arrangement using five different-colored crayons. Tell them that there are *many* possible arrangements. Ask them to find a few more of the arrangements.

Where's the Mathematics?

In this activity, children are involved in finding *permutations*, which are ordered arrangements of objects. Children record the ordered arrangements of four crayons of different colors. For children in primary grades, this activity calls for careful visual discrimination. Children must recognize, for example, that *blue-red-yellow-green* is different from *blue-red-green-yellow* and that both of these are different from *green-yellow-red-blue*.

For a crayon box with a row containing a red, a blue, a green, and a yellow crayon, there are 24 different arrangements.

red-blue-green-yellow	blue-red-green-yellow
red-blue-yellow-green	blue-red-yellow-green
red-green-blue-yellow	blue-green-red-yellow
red-green-yellow-blue	blue-green-yellow-red
red-yellow-blue-green	blue-yellow-red-green
red-yellow-green-blue	blue-yellow-green-red
green-red-blue-yellow	yellow-red-blue-green
green-red-yellow-blue	yellow-red-green-blue
green-blue-red-yellow	yellow-blue-red-green
green-blue-yellow-red	yellow-blue-green-red
green-yellow-red-blue	yellow-green-red-blue
green-yellow-blue-red	yellow-green-blue-red

Seeing so many arrangements may seem overwhelming to children until they begin to sort the crayon boxes. Children will notice that six boxes start with red, six with blue, six with green, and six with yellow. Next, they may focus on one set of boxes that starts with the same color, say blue. Of those six, two have red as the second color, two have green as the second color, and two have yellow as the second color. In the two boxes that start blue-red, the last two colors appear as green-yellow in one box and yellow-green in the other box. This same reversal of colors holds true for the boxes that start blue-green (red-yellow and yellow-red) or blue-yellow (red-green and green-red). Another way for children to see this pattern is to look at the six boxes that start with blue and notice that two of those boxes end with red

2. Have children find a possible arrangement using six different colored crayons. Tell them that there are *many* possible arrangements. Ask them to find a few more of the arrangements.

and that the two middle colors in each case are reversed. Helping them find patterns in what seems to be a totally random event helps children learn that these arrangements may often be predictable. Patterns can also help children to find any crayon-box arrangements that they might have missed in their Snap Cube modeling.

Children may find it especially interesting to compare their group's work to another group's in which the colors of the cubes used were not the same. The following information shows how dramatically the number of possible arrangements increases with the addition of each extra crayon color.

Number of Different-Colored Crayons in the Box	Number of Ways to Arrange Colors
1	1
2	2
3	6
4	24
5	120
6	720
7	5,040

To determine mathematically how many arrangements are possible, multiply the number of color choices for the first crayon (4) times the numbers of color choices for the second crayon (4 – 1) times the number of color choices for the third crayon (4 – 2), and so forth, until the box is full. The following calculation gives the possible number of arrangements for a box of four different-colored crayons:

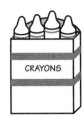

Crayon 1		Crayon 2		Crayon 3		Crayon 4	
4	×	(4 – 1)	×	(4 – 2)	×	(4 – 3)	
4	×	3	×	2	×	1	= 24

CLOSEST TO 100

Getting Ready

What You'll Need

Snap Cubes, 20 per team

Snap Cube sticks—each made up of 10 Snap Cubes of the same color, 10 per team

Closest to 100 game board, 1 per team, page 91

Die, 1 per group of teams

Snap Cube grid paper (optional), page 93

Overhead Snap Cubes and/or Snap Cube grid paper transparency (optional)

Overview

In this game for two to four teams of two players each, children choose single Snap Cubes or sticks of ten Snap Cubes according to the roll of a die. They position the cubes on a 100-grid in an effort to be the ones to come closest to covering the grid. In this activity, children have the opportunity to:

◆ work with place-value concepts

◆ estimate

◆ find two-digit sums

The Activity

You may wish to have children assemble the sticks of 10 Snap Cubes themselves prior to playing the game.

Introducing

◆ Show children a pile of single Snap Cubes and several sticks of 10 Snap Cubes. Have children count the cubes that make up a stick along with you to verify that there are ten.

◆ Display a sheet of Snap Cube grid paper. Call on a volunteer to roll a die and to announce the number that comes up. Have another volunteer place that many of the single cubes anywhere on the grid so that each cube lies within a grid square.

◆ Have other volunteers roll the die and place Snap Cubes on the grid until more than 10 cubes have been placed.

◆ Then tell children that you would like to trade some of the cubes on the grid for one of the Snap Cube sticks. Call on a volunteer to do this, then explain why the trade was fair.

◆ Play part of a game of *Closest to 100* with children before they begin *On Their Own*.

On Their Own

Play *Closest to 100!*

Here are the rules.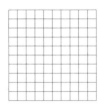

1. This is a game for a team of 2 players. Two or more teams play together. The object is to use Snap Cubes to cover as many squares as possible without going over 100 on a game board that looks like this:

2. Each team gets a game board. Teams take turns rolling 1 die. All teams use the same number rolled on each turn.

3. Each team takes as many single Snap Cubes or as many sticks of Snap Cubes as the number rolled. For example, if a 2 is rolled, a team may take 2 single Snap Cubes or 2 sticks of Snap Cubes.

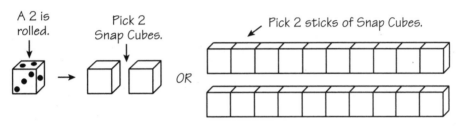

A 2 is rolled.   Pick 2 Snap Cubes.   Pick 2 sticks of Snap Cubes.

OR

4. Teams place the Snap Cubes or the sticks of Snap Cubes on their game boards. Whenever a team has 10 single Snap Cubes on the board, it must trade them for a Snap Cube stick.

5. The die may be rolled up to 6 times. Then the game must end.

6. Teams count how many cubes are on their grids and write that number down.

7. The team that comes closest to having 100 squares covered without going over 100 is the winner.

• Play several games of *Closest to 100*.

• Be ready to talk about good moves and bad moves.

The Bigger Picture

Thinking and Sharing

Invite children to talk about their games and some of the thinking they did.

Use prompts such as these to promote class discussion:

◆ What strategies did you and your partner use?

◆ Did any team cover exactly 100 squares?

◆ Which of your scores was closest to 100? How close was it?

◆ Who got a score that was far from 100? How far was it?

◆ What helped you decide whether to pick single cubes or cube sticks?

Writing and Drawing

Have children color a blank game board to show what it might look like if they rolled a 4, then a 3, then a 5. Have them compare their results, noting the number of cubes pictured and how far away that number is from 100.

Extending the Activity

1. Have children play the game in reverse by starting with 100 cubes on the game board. When they roll a die, they remove that number of cube

Teacher Talk

Where's the Mathematics?

This game gives children a visual experience with place value. If they roll a 3, for instance, they can clearly see the difference between how much of the game board could be covered by 3 single Snap Cubes and how much could be covered by 3 cube sticks (30 Snap Cubes). As the game continues, children get informal practice adding tens and ones to get a sum. They will see that adding additional sets of 10 does not change the number of ones. For example, if there are 22 Snap Cubes on the board and 3 sticks are added, this results in 52 cubes (5 sticks plus 2 singles). Children will see that the number of cube sticks has increased but the number of single cubes has remained at 2.

On the other hand, adding single cubes may have an impact on the number of cube sticks, as well as the number of ones. For example, if there are 37 Snap Cubes (3 sticks and 7 singles) on the board and 4 cubes are added, this will require a trade of 10 single cubes for a cube stick. This would result in 4 sticks and 1 single cube, changing both the number of cube sticks and the number of ones. Seeing how adding tens and ones affects the number of cube sticks and single cubes may help children form a mental picture of addition in their later work with algorithms. It may also strengthen their facility with mental math techniques.

As children gain experience with this game, they will see that they need to estimate. If children take too many tens, they will go over the target number, 100. If they take too many ones, they will not get close enough to 100. Partners must discuss the best way to optimize their chances of getting as close to 100 as possible without going over.

sticks or single cubes. At some point, they may have to trade a cube stick for 10 single cubes before they can complete their turn. After six rolls of the die, the team that is closest to having no cubes left on the board is the winner.

2. Have children work with a partner to figure out six rolls of the die that would give exactly 100 cubes. Ask them to write down what the rolls of the die would be and tell whether they should take cube sticks or single cubes with each roll.

There is no one best strategy for playing the game, and the children will probably have several different suggestions. Some that are typical are: "Take tens until you get past 50. Then be careful," "If the roll is a 3 or less, take tens," "Get to 80 by using tens as soon as you can. Then take ones," "If the other team is really close to 100, they might go over, so you can take ones and still be OK."

Watching their game boards fill up fast as they add cube sticks and slowly as they add single cubes will eventually help children predict which rolls of the die will help them in the latter part of the game. Some will enjoy keeping a running total of how many cubes are on the game board. Others will wait until the end of the game and then find the total. Some children will count by tens to facilitate finding the total.

When asked how close to 100 they got, many children will use the technique of "counting up" and simply count the number of blank spaces left on the board. Some may inadvertently think of this process in terms of both addition and its inverse, subtraction. For example, if 91 cubes were on the board, the child who counts up will discover that only 9 more are needed to get to get to 100; hence $91 + 9 = 100$. They may be encouraged to also view this situation as $100 - 91 = 9$ and thus be introduced to addition and subtraction as inverse operations.

Finally, children will see that covering exactly 100 squares is not easy. Most of the winning scores will be in the 90s with an occasional score in the 80s and few perfect 100s.

DIVIDING 24

Getting Ready

What You'll Need

Snap Cubes, 24 per pair
Small paper plates, 24 per pair
Overhead Snap Cubes (optional)

Overview

Children explore different ways that 24 Snap Cubes may be divided into equal-sized sets. In this activity, children have the opportunity to:

♦ view division as making same-sized sets

♦ recognize that a set may be divided in more than one way

The Activity

Introducing

♦ Display six Snap Cubes on a paper plate. Draw this on the chalkboard. Tell children to imagine that the cubes are small cakes. Say that this plate holds *one serving of six cakes*.

♦ Ask how the six cakes could be arranged on plates to make more than one serving. Explain that each serving must have the same number of cakes as the other servings.

♦ Have children use Snap Cubes and paper plates to show their solutions and explain why the servings are equal in size. Record pictures of their solutions on the board next to your drawing.

"Two servings of three cakes"

"Three servings of two cakes"

"Six servings of one cake"

♦ Establish that the six cakes cannot be arranged on plates to make 4 or 5 equal servings.

On Their Own

If you have 24 cakes, in how many different ways can you make equal servings?

- Work with a partner. Get 24 Snap Cubes to use as cakes. Get paper plates to hold the servings.

- Place all the Snap Cubes on plates so that the plates hold equal servings. Each plate must hold the same number of cakes. No cakes may be left over.

- Record what you did by drawing a picture of the plates of cakes.

- Now use a different number of plates to make equal servings from the 24 cakes. Record what you did.

- Continue to find and record ways to make equal servings until you think you have found them all.

- Look for patterns in your numbers of equal servings.

The Bigger Picture

Thinking and Sharing

When children think that they have found all the numbers of equal servings, call them together to share their findings. Ask volunteers to record a picture of one their solutions on the board. Continue until all the possibilities have been listed.

Use prompts such as these to promote class discussion:

- What is the greatest number of equal servings you could make? the least number?

- How do you know that you have found all of the possibilities?

- Do you see any patterns in the solutions?

- If you make two (three, four, and so forth) servings, what fractional part of the 24 cakes does each person get?

Drawing

Have children draw cakes on plates to show how they could arrange 12 cakes so that they and three friends would each have equal servings.

Extending the Activity

1. Have children identify how many cakes would be left over if 7, 9, 10, or 11 servings were made from 24 cakes.

2. Show three plates with six cubes on each plate. Ask children to look for other ways to arrange these cubes equally.

Where's the Mathematics?

The idea of sharing food with friends is a familiar one that children can relate to easily. This activity gives children an opportunity to connect the idea of sharing something fairly and equally with the concept of division.

Summarizing the data that children have collected helps children learn that one of mathematics' most powerful tools is organizing data so that patterns emerge. The summary could look like this:

Number of Servings	Serving Size
1	24 cakes
2	12 cakes
3	8 cakes
4	6 cakes
6	4 cakes
8	3 cakes
12	2 cakes
24	1 cake

Children will probably point out that, as the number of servings increases, the serving size decreases. Also, the columns showing the number of servings and serving sizes include the same numbers in reverse order. You may wish to introduce the word *factor* as the word used to describe the numbers that divide equally into another number. So, the factors of 24 are 1, 2, 3, 4, 6, 8, 12, and 24.

Organizing the data into a list such as the one above can help children see whether or not they have exhausted all the possibilities. For example, children may have found seven of the possible solutions, yet overlook one of them, such as 12 servings of 2. Seeing how the numbers in the list are reversals of each other could lead them to question whether 12 servings of 2 would be possible and then test it with their Snap Cubes. Children may also suggest that if five servings were a possibility, then the serving size would have to be 5 cakes in order for the numbers to fit into the list. Using Snap

Cubes or counting by 5s, they can eliminate this possibility when they wind up one cube short for the last plate. Using this same type of reasoning, if 7 servings were possible, the serving size would have to be between 3 and 4 and since the cubes cannot be cut, this is not possible.

You may like to informally introduce the concept of fractional parts of a whole set into the discussion. You might explain, for example, that if two servings are made, each person gets ½ of the 24, or 12 cakes. If three servings are made, each person gets ⅓ of the cakes, and so forth. Frequently, in the primary grades, the only model used to describe fractional parts is the area model like the one shown below.

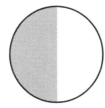

Half of the circle is shaded.

Modeling equal servings of cakes as done here introduces the concept of fractional parts of a set. Later, when children work with multiplying fractions, they will use this concept frequently in solving problems, such as ¼ x 24 = 6.

You may want to explore the idea of remainders as you ask children to think about what 5 equal servings would look like if they could cut the cakes and distribute the halves. Answers such as, "Each serving would have more than 4 cakes but less than 5 cakes," or "Each serving would be almost 5 cakes" would be very good answers and introduce the idea of number on a continuum rather than as discrete whole-number points on a number line.

HOW LONG IS IT?

- **Estimation**
- **Non-standard measurement**
- **Counting**
- **Subtraction**

Getting Ready

What You'll Need

Snap Cubes, about 40 per pair

How Long Is It? recording sheet, 1 per pair, page 92

Overview

Children estimate the length of various classroom objects in terms of Snap Cubes. Then they measure the objects with Snap Cube trains and compare their estimates to the actual measurements. In this activity, children have the opportunity to:

- ◆ work with non-standard measurement
- ◆ refine their ability to estimate length
- ◆ develop number sense

The Activity

Tell children that, in measuring length, they should ignore any posts that may stick out from the ends of the Snap Cube train.

Introducing

- ◆ Hold up one Snap Cube and a crayon. Ask children to think about how many cubes they would need to snap together to make a train equal in length to the crayon.

- ◆ Write these column headings on the board. Write the word *crayon* in the first column.

Object	Estimated Length	Actual Length
crayon		

- ◆ Call for some estimates of the length of the crayon. Write them in the second column.

- ◆ Invite a volunteer to snap some cubes together to make a train, placing it next to the crayon to show the actual length of the crayon in terms of Snap Cubes.

- ◆ Repeat the activity using another object.

On Their Own

How well can you estimate the length of an object?

- With a partner, choose an object in the classroom. Write the name of your object on part of a recording sheet that looks like this:

- Estimate how many Snap Cubes you would need to make a train the same length as your object. Record your estimate.

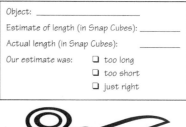

Object: _____

Estimate of length (in Snap Cubes): _____

Actual length (in Snap Cubes): _____

Our estimate was: ❑ too long
                     ❑ too short
                     ❑ just right

- Now measure your object with Snap Cubes. Do this by making a train and lining it up with your object. The number of Snap Cubes in the train is the actual length of your object. Record the actual length.

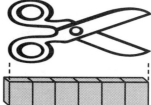

- Compare your estimate to the actual length. Check whether your estimate was too long, too short, or just right.

- Repeat the process of estimating, measuring, and comparing for several other objects. Each time, try to make a good estimate.

- Be ready to talk about your estimates.

The Bigger Picture

Thinking and Sharing

Ask volunteers to share one of the objects they measured. Invite the class to estimate its length in Snap Cubes and to explain how they made their estimates. Write the estimates on the board. Then have the volunteers reveal the actual length. Record this on the board as well. Repeat this process until all partners have had a chance to share one of their objects.

Use prompts such as these to promote class discussion:

- What makes a good estimate? What makes a bad estimate?

- Which estimates seemed reasonable? Why or why not?

- Which of the estimates were close to the actual measurement?

- How much longer (shorter) than the estimate was the actual measurement?

- Was it harder to estimate the length of an object that was very short or an object that was very long? Why do you think so?

- Did finding the actual length of your first object help you make an estimate for your next object? Explain.

- (Hold up an object.) Which object that we have already seen is probably closest in length to this object?

Drawing

Have children draw a picture of one of the objects they measured next to a Snap Cube train of the same length.

Where's the Mathematics?

This activity gives children an opportunity to practice estimation and measurement in an open-ended setting. The *Thinking and Sharing* gives children an opportunity to apply their newly practiced skills to a variety of objects that they have not yet measured. Listening to their peers explain why they chose a particular estimate can expose children to a number of different estimation techniques. It can also help children see that an estimate is based on reason and is not just a wild guess.

The measurements of many objects that children will choose will not be equal to an exact number of Snap Cubes. This can provide opportunities to discuss rounding the measurement to the length of the nearest Snap Cube or using a fraction to indicate measurement. Encourage children to use the method that makes the most sense to them. Answers such as "It is a little more than 8 Snap Cubes long" help set the stage for the need to introduce a new set of numbers, fractions, that will enable children to communicate about what "a little more than" means.

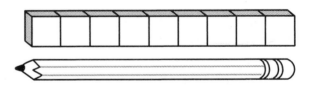

The pencil is a little longer than 9 cubes.

Children may give some of their estimates as a range of numbers. For example, an estimate such as, "The pen looks like it is about 7 to 9 Snap

Extending the Activity

Have children make a train of 20 Snap Cubes and then, without moving from their seats, identify two objects in the room each of which is about the length of their train. After they have identified the objects, have them measure them with their train to see if they were correct.

Cubes long" can take pressure off children who feel that if they estimate the pen to be 9 Snap Cubes long and the actual measurement is 8 Snap Cubes, then they have given a "wrong" estimate. Asking the question, "Which of the estimates were close to the actual measurement?" also encourages children to accept the idea that estimates only need to be "in the ballpark" to be good estimates.

When asked to compare their actual measurement to their estimate, children use subtraction. Some may subtract the numbers mentally. Others may build one train of Snap Cubes as long as their estimate and then another train of Snap Cubes as long as the actual measurement, finally lining up these two trains and "counting on" to find the difference in length.

Children also get chances to practice using the comparisons "longer" and "shorter" in context. If, after one child has shown that a calculator measures almost 6 Snap Cubes long and then a book is held up, observations might be made that the book is longer than the calculator and it looks as if two calculators laid end-to-end might be almost as long as the book. Hence, the book is probably "6 + 6 + one or two more," or 13 to 14 Snap Cubes long. Reasoning such as this helps children to develop a good number sense because they are fitting numbers together in meaningful contexts that may be verified concretely.

Children can also practice ordering numbers when they look at the list of objects and measurements on the board and put the items in order from shortest to longest. As the actual objects are placed in a line, children have verification that they are ordering the numbers correctly.

HOW MANY TRAINS?

- Patterns
- Counting
- Comparing
- Permutations

Getting Ready

What You'll Need

Snap Cubes, 5 each in 2 different colors per pair

Snap Cube grid paper, 1 sheet per pair, page 93

Overhead Snap Cubes and/or Snap Cube grid paper transparency (optional)

Overview

Children build as many three-cube trains as they can using no more than two colors of Snap Cubes. In this activity, children have an opportunity to:

- find all the possible arrangements for a given number of objects
- use record keeping to keep track of arrangements
- write equivalent number statements

The Activity

If possible, every pair of children should work with the same two colors of Snap Cubes in the On Their Own. This will help pairs to compare their results.

Introducing

- Place five red and five yellow Snap Cubes in front of you.
- Snap a red cube and a yellow cube together and show the train to the class. Hold up the train horizontally with the red cube on your right and explain that this is called a "red-yellow train" to describe the order of the colors.
- Snap two red cubes together and say that this is a "red-red train."
- Ask children to help you make other two-cube trains from the pile of two colors of cubes. Point out that even though two trains might have the same two color cubes, they are considered different trains if the order of the colors is different.
- Establish that different two-cube trains can be made: red-red, yellow-yellow, red-yellow, yellow-red. Demonstrate how to record these four trains by coloring in squares on Snap Cube grid paper.

On Their Own

How many different 3-cube trains can you make using up to 2 colors of Snap Cubes?

- With a partner, build a 3-cube train of Snap Cubes. Use up to 2 colors of cubes.

- Record your train.

- Now, build a different 3-cube train. One train is different from another if the order of the colors is different. These trains are different even though they both have 2 red cubes and 1 yellow cube.

```
R  Y  R        Y  R  R
```

- Record your second train.

- Continue to build and record trains until you think you have found them all.

- Be ready to tell how your trains are different from one another.

The Bigger Picture

Thinking and Sharing

Ask a volunteer to rebuild one of the trains he or she recorded and place it on display. Call on others to rebuild and show their trains until all the different trains that children found are on display.

Use prompts such as these to promote class discussion:

- ◆ (Hold up any two trains.) How are these two trains alike? How are they different?

- ◆ How could we fill in these blanks to make a number sentence that describes one of the trains?

$$\underline{\hspace{1.5cm}} + \underline{\hspace{1.5cm}} = \underline{\hspace{1.5cm}}$$
red   yellow   total
cube(s)   cube(s)   cubes

- ◆ How can we arrange our trains so that we know we have found all of them?

Drawing

Have children draw their 3-cube trains, "coupling" each to the next to form one long train. For example:

Then have them color their long train.

Extending the Activity

1. Have children make four- or five-cube trains of two colors each. They may record each train as they build it until they know they have made them all.

Where's the Mathematics?

There are eight three-cube trains that use no more than two colors. The first row below shows the trains that begin with red. The second row shows the trains that begin with yellow.

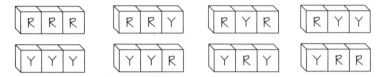

The mathematics behind the arrangements may be organized in something called a tree diagram. The tree below is a graphic representation of the color choices for the first, second, and third cubes.

There are two choices for the first cube: red or yellow. There are two choices for the second cube as well. So, a two-cube train would be red-red, red-yellow, yellow-red, or yellow-yellow. Each of these four possibilities again has two possibilities, red or yellow, when choosing the third cube. The final tree diagram is shown here. Following along each branching leads to one of the three-cube trains:

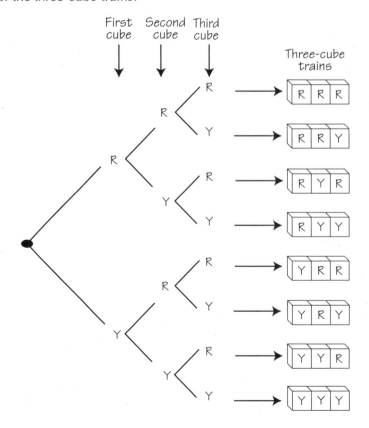

2. Have children build all the possible three-cube trains of up to three colors per train.

If you wanted to build a longer train, you could show it graphically by continuing to add two branches to each endpoint of the diagram tree.

The tree diagram indicates that the number of arrangements grows exponentially as the number of cubes in the arrangement grows. Children who build four- or five-cube trains of two colors will see that the number of possible arrangements will double with the addition of each extra cube to the train.

Trains Made from Two Colors of Cubes	
Number of cubes in the train	Number of ways to arrange cubes
1	2
2	4
3	8
4	16
5	32
6	64
7	128

After you have exhausted a discussion of all the possible ordered arrangements, you may wish to extend the learning in this lesson by having the children complete number sentences for each train using this format:

$$\underline{\qquad} + \underline{\qquad} = \underline{\qquad}$$
red yellow total
cube(s) cube(s) cubes

This will give children practice in seeing multiple ways of expressing one sum as well as highlighting that zero can be a possible addend.

This lesson previews a probability concept called permutations. Permutations are ordered arrangements of objects. In this activity, children record the ordered arrangements of Snap Cubes. In other settings, this same idea of ordering is used when recording the outcomes of flipping a coin, looking at the possible distribution of boys and girls in a family, or studying the appearance of dominant and recessive genes in biology.

MAKE A COPY

Getting Ready

What You'll Need

Snap Cubes, 24 per pair

Books or heavyweight folders to use as barriers

Overhead Snap Cubes and/or Snap Cube grid paper transparency (optional)

Overview

Children build a Snap Cube structure and describe it to a partner so that the partner can build an identical structure. In this activity, children have the opportunity to:

- ◆ discover the importance of using accurate mathematical vocabulary
- ◆ follow verbal directions
- ◆ improve their listening and visualization skills

The Activity

You might like to write the words and/or phrases children suggest, such as "a tree shape," "on top of," "in a straight line," and "ten cubes," on the chalkboard.

Introducing

- ◆ Build a Snap Cube structure like the one shown. Keep it hidden.
- ◆ Tell children that you have made a structure which you will show to them later. Explain that their job is to build a copy of your structure according to the directions you will give them.
- ◆ Give step-by-step directions for building the structure.
- ◆ When everyone is ready, show your structure and have children compare theirs to yours.
- ◆ Ask the class to identify the words or phrases you used in your directions that helped them visualize the structure.

©1996 Cuisenaire Company of America, Inc.

On Their Own

> **How can you describe a Snap Cube structure you have made so that your partner can make it, too?**
>
> - Work with a partner. Decide who will build the structure and give the directions, and who will follow the directions. Set up a barrier so that neither of you can see the other's workspace.
>
> - Build a structure using 8 to 12 Snap Cubes.
>
> - Give directions for building your structure one step at a time.
>
> - Your partner listens to your directions and tries to build a structure that exactly matches yours. Your partner may ask questions.
>
> - When all the directions have been followed, remove the barrier. Are the structures exactly the same? If not, discuss why.
>
> - Switch roles and try the activity again.

The Bigger Picture

Thinking and Sharing

Ask children to describe what happened during the activity. Invite pairs of volunteers to discuss how successful they were in building matching structures.

Use prompts such as these to promote class discussion:

- Was it easier to build and give directions or to follow directions? Why?

- What kinds of things were hardest to describe? What kinds of things were easiest to describe?

- Were there any words that you found to be useful in your descriptions or in your questions? Explain.

- What tips would you give to another child who builds a structure and gives the directions? to another child who follows the directions?

- If you did the activity again, what would you do differently?

Drawing

Give children the opportunity to draw their favorite structure. The structure may be one that they themselves designed or one that they built from their partner's directions.

Extending the Activity

1. Ask children to repeat the activity, but this time the partner following the directions may ask only *yes* or *no* questions.

Teacher Talk

Where's the Mathematics?

This activity may be difficult for some children since it relies on the vocabulary expertise of the child creating the structure and his or her ability to organize directions in a sequence that makes sense. It relies as well on the listening and interpreting skills of the builder. Because children are just developing these skills, you can use this activity over and over again to assess growth in both vocabulary and comprehension.

Many children assume that others understand what they say; that is, that others attach the same meaning to the same set of words. Younger children especially will have difficulty getting their partners to build their structure exactly. They may identify the structure by some common name, such as "tree" or "frog" to assist in the process. However, "tree" or "frog" are ambiguous terms. Backing up these words with more precise, less subjective language is an important facet of communicating mathematically. For example, merely describing the structure used in the *Introducing* section as a "tree" could lead to different interpretations such as these:

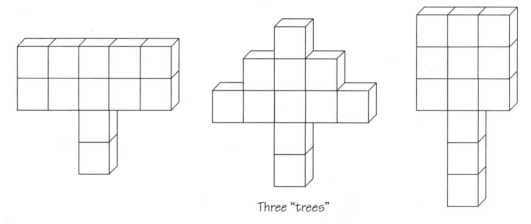

Three "trees"

Relating numbers and colors can contribute a great deal to conveying a visual image to the person who is following the directions. For example, the "tree" in the *Introducing* section might be described this way: "It has 9 green cubes and 1 brown cube for the trunk. The bottom row of the tree has 5 cubes. The row above that has 3 cubes placed over the 2nd, 3rd, and 4th cubes of the bottom row. Then, 1 cube placed right in the middle forms the top row. The brown trunk is located under the 3rd cube of the bottom row." This description uses both cardinal numbers—9, 5, 3, and 1—to describe how many and ordinal numbers—2nd, 3rd, and 4th—to show location. This description also points out how it is easier to describe a complex figure by describing its parts (each row of the tree) instead of the whole.

2. Have children work with their partners to build a structure and write a set of directions that could be used to build it. Have pairs exchange directions and try to build each other's structures.

A good description includes words that indicate direction, such as *under, over, on top, right, left, bottom, top,* and some words that indicate shape, such as *rectangle, square,* or *triangle.* Young children may use body language, as well. For instance, instead of saying "right," a child might say, "Put two cubes on this side" and wave his or her right hand in the air to underscore what is meant by "this side." If children are sitting across from each other rather than side-by-side, this use of body language may actually lead the listener to put the two cubes on the left, rather than on the right.

The opportunity to use mathematical language in context is crucial in the construction of mathematical understanding. Mathematical terms such as *ten, third, between,* and *next to* provide children with the means to give a more precise description of a structure. It is a good idea to keep a running list of mathematical terms on a large chart for all to see and refer to. This list should be compiled as the terms emerge in context and become part of the dialogue. In this way, the word is connected to an experience, helping to make discussion of the term meaningful. In addition, a picture or diagram drawn next to some terms on the list provides a good visual reference.

In comparing their two structures, children have an opportunity to deepen their understanding of congruence. Children may need to scrutinize their structures carefully to determine whether or not they are identical and, if not, how they differ. The two structures may be congruent, but if the structures have to be flipped or rotated to match, they would not be identical.

The task of comparing structures provides immediate feedback for the partners on how well they were able to communicate with each other. Children should be encouraged to try to figure out which descriptions may have been misinterpreted and to discuss better ways of explaining or describing those particular attributes of the structures.

Children should recognize that the goal of the direction giver is not to try to trick the listener, but rather to provide useful descriptions that will enable the listener to build an exact copy of the direction giver's structure. This is not a competitive game. The importance of the skills brought to the task by both partners—describing, listening, visualizing, and questioning—become more and more evident as children repeat the activity and take turns at the two roles.

MIRRORED IMAGES

Getting Ready

What You'll Need

Snap Cubes, 12 each of 2 different colors per child

Snap Cube grid paper, page 93

Overhead Snap Cubes and/or Snap Cube grid paper transparency (optional)

Overview

Children build a Snap Cube structure, place it along the fold of a piece of grid paper, trace around it, and cut out the shape to create a symmetrical design. Then they challenge their partner to create the mirrored image of their structure. In this activity, children have the opportunity to:

- work with line symmetry
- create a symmetrical design using folded paper
- build a mirrored image of a design

The Activity

If symmetry is a new topic for children, explain that an object has line symmetry if it can be folded along a line and the sides fold over each other exactly.

Introducing

- Display a one-layer design made from six Snap Cubes of one color.
- Fold a piece of Snap Cube grid paper in half along one of the grid lines.
- Place the Snap Cube design on the grid so that the edges of some of the cubes lie along the fold.
- Trace around the design.
- Keeping the paper folded, cut out the design.
- Unfold the cutout design.
- Place the Snap Cube design on one side of the fold. Call on a volunteer to use Snap Cubes to create a design that would fit on the other side of the fold. Explain that the two designs are mirrored images of each other and that the fold line between them is a *line of symmetry*.

On Their Own

Can you create a mirrored image of a Snap Cube design?

- Work with a partner. Each of you use up to 12 Snap Cubes to create a 1-layer design. Place your design flat on a table so that all the cubes touch the table.

- Use your Snap Cube design to make a paper design that has a line of symmetry. Here's how:
    - Place your Snap Cube design on a folded piece of grid paper so that the edges of some of the cubes touch the fold.
    - Trace around the design.
    - Keeping the paper folded, cut out the design. Do not cut along the fold line.

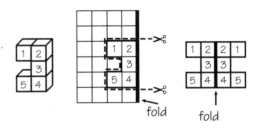

Symmetry with 5 Snap Cubes

- Keep your cut-out paper design hidden from your partner.

- Exchange Snap Cube designs with your partner. Tell each other which Snap Cubes you placed along the fold of the paper design.

- Challenge your partner to build the mirrored image of your Snap Cube design. The mirrored image is the Snap Cube design that would fit exactly on the other side of the fold on the paper design.

- Check each other's work by placing each Snap Cube design with its mirrored image on the paper design.

The Bigger Picture

Thinking and Sharing

Put the Snap Cube designs on display and ask for volunteers to match them up with the paper designs.

Use prompts such as these to promote class discussion:

- How did you know how to build the mirrored image of your partner's design?
- What helped you match up the paper design with the Snap Cube design?
- How would the paper design change if a different part of the Snap Cube design touched the fold?
- Can you find anything else in the classroom that has a line of symmetry? Explain.

Extending the Activity

1. Have children investigate how the paper cut-out changes when they place different sides of the Snap Cube design along the fold line.

Where's the Mathematics?

Frequently, lessons about symmetry ask children to look at an object or picture and identify where the line of symmetry is located. This lesson, on the other hand, has children build a shape and then use that shape to build a symmetrical design by building its mirrored image.

Many children will build mirrored images using a trial-and-error method, eyeballing their work as they go along. Others will devise more specific methods. One such method would be based on the way the paper design was created: children build an exact copy of the original design, place it on top of the original design to check for accuracy, and then flip over the copy and place it beside the original design.

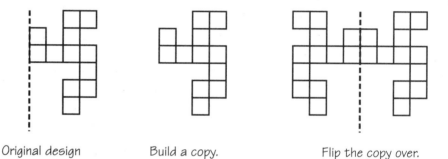

Original design   Build a copy.   Flip the copy over.
                                                 Place it beside the original.

Other children prefer to use a process of counting cubes to determine the placement of cubes in the mirrored image. For example, some children would look at the original design below and identify the four-cube horizontal piece as a strong design element, so they would put that in place first. Then, noting that the first cube to the right of the line of symmetry has one cube sitting on top of it, they would put one cube on top of the first cube to the left of the symmetry line. Since there are two cubes on top of the third cube to the right of the line of symmetry, they would put two cubes on top of the third cube to the left, and so on.

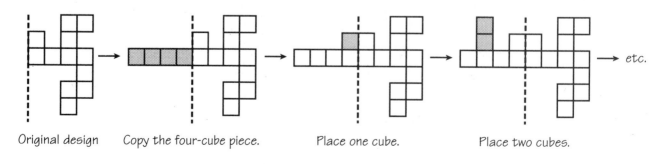

Original design   Copy the four-cube piece.   Place one cube.   Place two cubes.

2. Have children begin a paper design with two-line symmetry by folding the paper into fourths. After they build their Snap Cube design, that have them position it on the grid paper so that parts of it touch both the folds. Then have them trace and cut out their design.

Children do not need to be able to articulate "left" and "right" or "first" and "third" to be able to apply this kind of thinking. More likely, they are thinking, "I have to do the same thing, but on the other side" and then they merely count to determine the placement of the cubes.

Some children will experience more difficulty if they try to build a mirrored image along a horizontal line of symmetry than if they try to build it along a vertical line of symmetry. This is probably because more objects, both naturally occurring and manufactured, exhibit vertical lines of symmetry, and so the eye is more familiar with making left-right shifts across a line of symmetry. If this is a difficulty for children, they can easily rotate the Snap Cube design so that the line of symmetry has a vertical orientation.

Asking the question, "How would the paper design change if a different part of the Snap Cube design touched the fold?" can lead to some interesting changes in design, as shown in the seven-cube design below. Some children will have discovered this idea on their own if they did not listen carefully when their partner told them where the line of symmetry was located or if their partner incorrectly identified which side of the structure had been placed against the fold. Here are some outcomes for a seven-cube design.

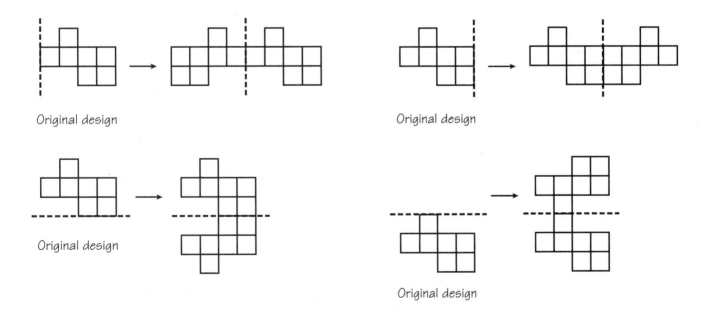

Original design

Original design

Original design

Original design

MULTIPLES OF TEN

Getting Ready

What You'll Need

Snap Cubes, 10 to 100 per child depending on the number drawn

Multiples-of-Ten slips, page 94

Paper bag to hold a set of Multiples-of-Ten slips

Large cards (10) each with a multiple of ten, from 10 to 100, written on it

Overview

Children build Snap Cube structures using multiples of 10 and then order the structures according to the number of cubes from which they were built. In this activity, children have the opportunity to:

♦ count out large and small quantities of objects

♦ work with multiples of 10

♦ develop number sense about the relative magnitude of numbers

♦ work with conservation of number

The Activity

Introducing

♦ Display the ten large cards showing the multiples of ten. Then put the card showing 50 in the middle of the chalk tray.

♦ Now tell children that you need their help to organize the cards in numerical order, from smallest to largest.

♦ Give any card to a volunteer and ask him or her to place it in order on the chalk tray. Point out that they need to leave enough room between cards to fit in any missing numbers. When everyone in the class agrees that the card has been placed correctly, ask the class to identify the missing multiples needed to fit between the two numbers.

♦ Give any other card to a second volunteer. Repeat the process until the cards are all lined up correctly.

©1996 Cuisenaire Company of America, Inc.

On Their Own

> **Can you build a Snap Cube structure and keep the number of cubes you used a secret?**
>
> - With a partner, pick a number slip from the bag. Agree to keep your number a secret from the rest of the class.
>
> - Each of you count out enough Snap Cubes to match your secret number.
>
> - Each of you build a structure using all the Snap Cubes you counted out.
>
> - Fold the slip along the dotted line. Cut it or tear it apart so that you both have a copy of the number.
>
> - Your teacher will tell you where to place your structure. Hide the slip with your secret number under the structure.
>
> - Now, pick another slip and repeat the activity for that number of Snap Cubes.

The Bigger Picture

Thinking and Sharing

Call children together and discuss how they went about building their structures.

Use prompts such as these to promote class discussion:

- Which structures do you think used 10 Snap Cubes? How can you tell?

- Which structures do you think used 100 Snap Cubes? How can you tell?

- (Point to a structure.) Do you think this structure used a number of Snap Cubes closer to 10, closer to 100, or just about in the middle? Why?

- (Pointing to two of the structures.) One of these structures used 80 cubes and one used 40. Which do you think used 40 cubes? Why?

- This structure (pointing to one) used either 30, 60, or 90 Snap Cubes. Which do you think it is? Why?

- This structure (pointing to one) used 60 Snap Cubes. Which other structures look as if they used about 60 cubes, too?

- How could you go about putting all these structures in order?

As children identify the number of Snap Cubes used in a particular structure, pick up the structure and reveal the secret number underneath.

Extending the Activity

Have children discuss which structures they could combine to create structures that are built from other numbers of Snap Cubes, such as 150 or 200.

Where's the Mathematics?

This activity encourages children to focus on the relative magnitude of the multiples of ten from 10 through 100. Children create a visual display of magnitude as they line up the structures in order, from those made from 10 Snap Cubes to those made from 100 Snap Cubes. Counting out the cubes gives them practice using greater numbers. Seeing the number cards marked 10, 20, 30, ..., 100 gives children additional exposure to the order of the base-ten number system.

It should be fairly easy for children to identify structures that use only 10 or 20 Snap Cubes since they can just look for the smallest structures or count the number of Snap Cubes they see. When two structures are built from the same number of cubes, children can compare how different they look. For example, both of the structures below are made from 10 Snap Cubes. The one on the left, which is built to look like a snake with its head raised, may seem to children as if it contains more Snap Cubes than the one on the right, which is built to look like a person.

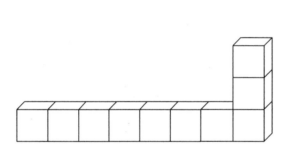 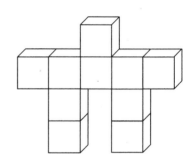

This contrast of a long, skinny line of cubes versus a more compact arrangement can be even more dramatic when the structures are made from greater numbers of Snap Cubes. Discussing how the eye may be fooled by such arrangements is often interesting for young children. As the ordered arrangement of structures is filled in, children see examples of how the same number of cubes can produce structures that look very different. This is similar to learning that a short, wide glass can hold just as much water as can a tall, skinny glass. Identifying the structures that use 100 Snap Cubes may be more difficult since this number cannot be easily counted just by looking at the structure. But once you have two of the smallest and largest structures—those made from 10 cubes and those made from 100 cubes—in place, children can start to develop a feel for how other structures fit into the continuum.

Distinguishing between a structure that used 40 cubes and another one that used 50 cubes is probably too fine a distinction for most children, but they can certainly be expected to identify that neither of these structures used just 10 or as many as 100 cubes. Estimating that a structure uses somewhere between 40 and 70 cubes would be reasonable and would demonstrate that the child is developing a good number sense.

The questions: (Pointing to two of the structures) "One of these structures used 80 cubes and one used 40. Which do you think used 40 cubes? Why?" or "This structure (pointing to one) used either 30, 60, or 90 Snap Cubes. Which do you think it is? Why?" help children to focus on the sorting and ordering, but still require critical thinking. To answer the first question, children may begin to understand not only that 80 is greater than 40, but that 80 is twice 40. To answer the second question, children will likely think about the relative magnitudes of 30, 60, and 90.

ON THE METER MARK

- Counting
- Probability
- Mental math

Getting Ready

What You'll Need

Snap Cubes, about 60 in 2 different colors per pair

Dice, 2 per pair

Meter stick or 1-meter length of masking tape marked off on the floor, 1 per pair

Meter Mark recording sheet, page 95

Snap Cube grid paper, page 93

Overview

Children build Snap Cube trains that are at least one meter long by repeatedly rolling a pair of dice to find the number of cubes to add to the train. In this activity, children have the opportunity to:

- practice counting
- investigate the probability of rolling the various sums on a pair of dice

The Activity

Introducing

- Prepare a Snap Cube meter stick, but keep it hidden. The stick should have 52 cubes arranged in a long train to look like this:

| 10 red | 10 yellow | 10 blue | 10 green | 10 white | 2 black |

- Show the class an actual meter stick and one Snap Cube.
- Ask children to guess how many Snap Cubes would be needed to make a train as long as the meter stick.
- As volunteers explain their guesses, record them on the board.
- Reveal your Snap Cube meter stick and hold it up against the actual meter stick. Explain that each of the big sections of one color contains 10 Snap Cubes.
- Have the class count with you to confirm the number of cubes in each section and to establish that the Snap Cube meter stick is made up of 52 Snap Cubes.

On Their Own

How many rolls of a pair of dice will it take to make a Snap Cube train that is at least 1 meter long?

- Work with a partner. Decide which color of Snap Cubes each of you will use.
- One of you rolls the dice and finds the sum. Use your cubes to make a train to match the sum. Put the train next to the "0" point on the meter stick.
- The other of you rolls the dice and finds the sum. Make a train using your color of cubes. Snap this train onto your partner's train.
- Take turns rolling the dice and adding to the train until it is at least as long as the meter stick.
- For each train, record your sums, how many cubes are in your train, and how many times the dice were rolled. Use an outline that looks like this: Then take your train apart.

  Record the sums: _____
  How many cubes in the train? _____
  How many rolls did it take? _____

- Repeat the activity as many times as you can. Save the last train that you make.
- Study all of your recording sheets. Look for patterns in your data.

The Bigger Picture

Thinking and Sharing

Invite children to compare their trains and their data. Suggest that they make a class graph to show how many rolls it took to build a train at least as long as a meter stick. Set up the graph by writing the numbers 1 to 26 across the bottom of the chalkboard. Then, as each pair calls out the number of rolls needed for each of their trains, mark an "X" above the corresponding numbers.

Use prompts such as these to promote class discussion:

- How were your final trains the same? How were they different?
- What patterns did you notice in your data?
- What was the least number of rolls you needed? What was the greatest number of rolls?
- What information did you learn from the class graph?

Drawing

Have children tape sheets of Snap Cube grid paper together and draw a picture of a Snap Cube train that has exactly 52 cubes. Then have them color their train to indicate possible sums of the rolls of a pair of dice that could have resulted in the train.

Teacher Talk

Where's the Mathematics?

On the Meter Mark has a lesson on probability embedded in an activity that provides children with many opportunities to count, add, and tally results. As soon as they roll the dice, children need to find a sum. Some children will find the sum using mental math. Other children who do not have the sums committed to memory will be able to build the sum by making two trains, each equivalent in length to the number on a die, and then combining them and counting up to the find the sum. Children receive reinforcement on the addition facts by modeling the sums with the Snap Cube trains. When asked to record the number of rolls required to build the meter stick, some children will count the number of times the colors alternated while others may use tally marks to keep track of each partner's turn.

Sums of 6, 7, and 8 come up more frequently than do other sums because there are more combinations that can produce them. A sum of 2 is only possible one way—by rolling a 1 on each die. A sum of 12 is only possible by rolling a 6 on each die. In contrast, there are six ways to roll a 7: 1 + 6, 6 + 1, 2 + 5, 5 + 2, 3 + 4, and 4 + 3. As children work, they intuitively recognize that some sums are more likely to occur than others. You can build on this intuition during class discussion by asking for a show of hands to indicate who got a certain sum during the last game played. You should get more responses for sums of 6, 7, and 8 than for sums of 2 and 12.

When asked for the least and greatest number of rolls it took to build the meter stick, children are likely to report the numbers from their collected data. Theoretically, a meter stick could be completed in as few as 5 rolls of the dice, especially if a sum of 12 occurred several times; and theoretically, it could take as many as 26 rolls of the dice to complete the meter stick if sums of 2 were consistently rolled. In practice, however, most meter sticks will be completed in 7 to 10 rolls.

When children compare their Snap Cube trains, they are likely to notice that many have the same number of color alternations, but the sums that make

Extending the Activity

1. Have children investigate how many ways seven rolls of the dice could give a total of 52. Have them repeat this investigation for other numbers of rolls.

2. Have children repeat the activity using three die. Then ask them to compare the data to the data they found using two die.

---

up the turns vary. For example, each of these Snap Cube trains took 7 rolls to complete, but the sums on the rolls varied as did the total lengths.

$$8 + 10 + 4 + 5 + 10 + 9 + 11 = 57$$

$$4 + 8 + 12 + 9 + 5 + 12 + 5 = 55$$

Other trains that are exactly the same length may require a different number of rolls to complete. For example, the train below has 57 cubes—just like the first stick shown above—but it took 8 rolls of the dice to complete.

$$7 + 5 + 8 + 6 + 3 + 9 + 9 + 10 = 57$$

Children are likely to point out that many small sums, such as 3s and 4s, will take more turns to complete the stick than when large sums, such as 9 and 10, are rolled. Observations such as this one contribute to developing strong number sense.

Pooling their data to create one large class graph allows children to spot trends they may not have seen if they played the game only a few times and examined only their own data. The class graph will probably have the tallest columns of data for the range of 7 to 10 rolls, with smaller columns of data on either side of this range.

Working alongside the meter stick provides a subtle reinforcement of the number line, with its demarcations in groups of ten and repetitions of the numbers 1 to 9 between those demarcations.

PUZZLES

- Counting
- Estimation
- Area
- Comparing

Getting Ready

What You'll Need

Snap Cubes, 30 per pair

Puzzle Shapes, pages 96-100

Construction paper, 14 sheets

Snap Cube grid paper, page 93

Overhead Snap Cubes and/or Snap Cube grid paper transparency (optional)

Overview

Children estimate, then find the number of Snap Cubes required to cover the areas of figures. In this activity, children have the opportunity to:

- find the area of a variety of shapes
- discover that different shapes may have the same area
- develop estimation skills
- develop and use systems for counting groups of numbers

The Activity

After copying the five Puzzle Shapes *pages, cut the 14 puzzle shapes out and mount each one on construction paper for children to use in* On Their Own.

You may need to point out that, as children cover the puzzle shapes, they should ignore the connectors on the ends of the Snap Cubes that lie beyond the outlines of the shapes.

Introducing

- Show children one of the *Puzzle Shapes* worksheets. Ask them for estimates of how many Snap Cubes will cover the shape.
- Place cubes on the shape.
- With the help of the class, count the number of Snap Cubes needed to cover the shape.
- Explain that the word "area" is used to describe the number of Snap Cubes needed to cover the shape and that the area of this figure is equal to ——— Snap Cubes.

On Their Own

How many puzzle shapes can you find that have the same area?

- Work with a partner and take 1 of the puzzle shapes from the classroom set.

- Estimate how many Snap Cubes would completely cover the shape.

- Then place Snap Cubes on the shape to find the area. The area of the shape is the number of Snap Cubes that will exactly cover the shape. For example, this shape has an area of 12 Snap Cubes.

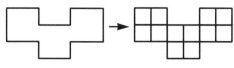
Area = 12 Snap Cubes

- Compare your estimate to the actual area of the puzzle shape.

- Record your results by copying the picture you see on the shape. Write the area of the shape next to the picture.

- Return the puzzle shape to the classroom set. Choose another shape that you think has the same area as your first shape. Find and record the area of this shape.

- Continue to choose shapes and find their areas. Check your results to see if any of the shapes have the same area.

- Keep looking until you find at least 1 pair of shapes with the same area. Look for shortcuts for finding area.

The Bigger Picture

Thinking and Sharing

Write children's findings on the board. You might use sentences like this: Each of shapes ☐ and shape Ⓧ have an area of 23 Snap Cubes.

You may want to post the puzzle shapes for reference.

Use prompts such as these to promote class discussion:

- How did you find the area of these shapes?

- How close were your estimates to the actual areas?

- (Point to one figure.) How would you estimate the area of this figure?

- How could you tell which puzzle shape has the greatest area without using cubes?

- What ideas do you have for counting the cubes?

Writing

Have children use Snap Cubes to create two different shapes that would each cover an area of 15 Snap Cubes. Then have them trace the figures onto Snap Cube grid paper and explain why they know each area is 15.

Extending the Activity

1. Have children add to the class collection by making two new shapes that look different but have the same area. Have them keep track of the areas of the new shapes.

2. Take one shape of each area from the classroom set of puzzles. Have children put them in order of area, from smallest to largest.

Teacher Talk

Where's the Mathematics?

This activity gives children opportunities to see that shapes that look different may have the same area. Children use estimation to predict the area of a shape based on their understanding of the size of the face of a Snap Cube. They use estimation again as they look through the class set of puzzles for shapes with matching areas.

Children's early estimates will probably be just guesses. As they find the areas of more shapes, they begin to develop estimation strategies. As they share their estimation strategies and listen to the strategies of their classmates, they start to see that estimates are more than mere guesses. Some estimation strategies may include comparing a shape to one whose area they have already found or noting that certain longer figures may have areas that are close to those of more compact figures.

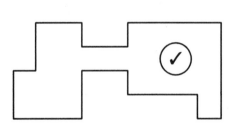 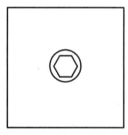

Many children simply count the Snap Cubes to find area. However, some may discover that counting in groups can save time. For example, in this figure, children who focus on columns will see four 2s, four 3s, and two 4s. Those who focus on rows will see one 2, one 6, and two 10s.

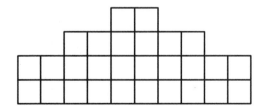

3. Show the children a puzzle shape that they have not seen before. Have them compare the shape to other puzzle shapes whose areas they have already figured out. Ask questions about the new shape such as, "Is it larger? smaller?" and "How is it the same? different?" Ask children to use the answers to these questions to estimate the area. Then have them use Snap Cubes to find the actual area.

Some children may develop visual means of recognizing groups of numbers. For example, they may organize their Snap Cubes in rows (or columns) of different colors to facilitate finding area. The child who covered the shape shown below arranged the cubes into trains of four of one color and three of another color. This allows for skip-counting by 4s (4, 8, **12**), then by 3s (3, 6, **9**), then adding to find the area (12 + 9 = 21).

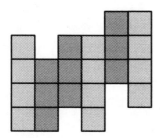

Other children may use a marker cube in a different color to keep track of each tenth cube they have counted.

1	2	3	4						
5	6	7	8	9		1	2	3	4
	5	6	7	8	9		1	2	3

Not all children are comfortable with the place-value concepts that can help them with their counting. These children will need many experiences with grouping sets of ten cubes before they are convinced that, for example, two groups of ten and one group of twenty represent the same number.

RED OR BLUE?

Getting Ready

What You'll Need

Snap Cubes, 15 red and 20 blue per pair

Paper bags to hold Snap Cubes, 1 per pair

Overview

In this game for two players, children draw Snap Cubes from a bag and collect the cubes according to the color they have been assigned. The first child to collect ten cubes wins. In this activity, children have the opportunity to:

◆ explore concepts of probability

◆ conclude whether or not a game is fair

The Activity

You may want to fill the paper bags with cubes (as indicated above) at this time for children's use in On Their Own.

Introducing

◆ Ask children to explain what it means for a game to be *fair*.

◆ Then ask children to explain what it means for a game to be *unfair*.

◆ Have children name some of their favorite games and tell whether they think each one is fair or not.

◆ Discuss which kind of game—fair or unfair—is more fun to play.

On Their Own

Play *Red or Blue?*

Here are the rules.

1. This is a game for 2 players. The object is to be the first player to collect either 10 red Snap Cubes or 10 blue Snap Cubes.

2. Players decide who will collect red cubes and who will collect blue cubes. They take turns drawing a cube from the bag without peeking into it.

3. If the cube picked is red, it goes to the player collecting red cubes. If the cube picked is blue, it goes to the player collecting blue cubes.

4. The first player to collect 10 cubes is the winner.

- Who won, red or blue?

- Return the cubes to the bag and play *Red or Blue?* several more times. For each game, switch colors and keep track of which color wins.

- Without looking into the bag, decide whether or not this game is fair.

The Bigger Picture

Thinking and Sharing

Discuss whether or not children think the game is fair. Do not let them look at the contents of the bag yet. You may wish to collect the class data in a chart like this:

Who won?	How many times?
Blue	𝍅𝍅𝍅 I
Red	𝍅 I

After children have discussed what they see in the chart, have them spill the contents of the bag onto their desks.

Use prompts such as these to promote class discussion:

- Which color would you rather collect—red or blue? Why?

- Do you think the game is fair? Explain.

- Why is making a class tally useful in determining whether the game is fair?

- What can we learn from the class tally?

- Why do you think blue wins more often?

- How could you change the game to make it fair?

- How could you change the game to make it more likely for red to win?

Extending the Activity

1. Have children play the game again, this time using the modifications they suggested for making the game fair or for making it more likely for red to win. Have them keep track of who wins, then analyze the data to see if the outcome matched their expectations.

Teacher Talk

Where's the Mathematics?

Children often discuss the issue of fairness. This activity is a simple game that may be easily varied to favor one player or the other or to give both players equally likely chances of winning. The game goes quickly, allowing a lot of data to be collected in a short amount of time. As the game is described with 15 red and 20 blue cubes in the paper bag, blue has the advantage since there is one-third more blue cubes in the bag than red cubes. Blue will win more often since it will be easier to collect ten blue cubes. On the average, ten blue cubes will be collected in the same amount of time it takes six or seven red cubes to be collected.

Once children have seen that blue seems to win repeatedly, they will probably report that they would want to play blue. However, some children will still hold out and report that they want to play red because red is their favorite color and they have a hard time letting go of their personal favorites despite the data that favors blue. Some children will also report that the game is fair despite evidence to the contrary because they expect that any situations that the teacher sets up will be fair.

Making the class tally allows the class to pool its data and see trends that might not appear in a small data set. It also makes the data a little less per-

2. Have children design a similar game for three or four players. Allow them to decide whether to make their game either fair or unfair.

sonal so that children may more willingly give up false perceptions. Using tally marks demonstrates the efficiency of counting by fives. Giving children a chance to analyze data that they have generated and collected themselves is empowering and gives them a true sense of what mathematicians do when confronted with problems.

When asked why blue is more likely to win, some children will not be able to articulate an explanation. Other children will attribute blue's winning entirely to chance. Some children will correctly deduce that there are more blue cubes than red cubes in the bag. Revealing the contents of the bag will affirm this. For children who did not have any opinions on why blue won more frequently, seeing the evidence of what is in the bag is apt to be greeted with cries of "You tricked us!" As soon as most children see the unequal mix of blue and red, they understand why the game favors blue.

Asking children to offer suggestions for how to make the game fair or how to make the game favor red provides a good opportunity to assess whether children understand how the ratio of cubes affects the probability of the color drawn from the bag and, hence, the final outcome of the game.

SHOWING ONE HALF

- Fractions
- Counting
- Comparing
- Sorting

Getting Ready

What You'll Need

Snap Cubes, 50 per pair in 2 different colors

Die, 1 per pair

Snap Cube grid paper, page 93

Overhead Snap Cubes and/or Snap Cube grid paper transparency (optional)

Overview

Children use two different colors of Snap Cubes to build a design in which each colored section represents one half of the design. In this activity, children have an opportunity to:

- ◆ develop an understanding of the meaning of one half
- ◆ discover that there are many ways to show one half
- ◆ see that the two halves of a whole have equal areas

The Activity

Introducing

- ◆ Roll a die and take as many red Snap Cubes as the number rolled.
- ◆ Ask a volunteer to take that same number of Snap Cubes in a different color.
- ◆ Arrange all the Snap Cubes into a design that is one layer high. Ask if anyone can explain why you can describe your arrangement as "half red."
- ◆ After listening to children's responses, count the cubes in the design aloud, pointing out the total number of cubes, the number of red cubes, and the number of the other-colored cubes. Explain that whenever a design has the same number of cubes in one color as in another color, the design is made up of one half of each color.

On Their Own

How can you build a Snap Cube design that is half one color and half another color?

- Work with a partner. Each of you choose a different color of Snap Cube.

- Roll the die. Each of you count out that many Snap Cubes of your color.

- Put your Snap Cubes together to make a design. Make sure your design is in 1 layer. When you place the design on a table, the Snap Cubes must all touch the table.

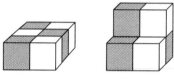

Okay   Not okay

- Think about why your design shows one half of each color. Then set it aside.

- Continue to roll the die and use Snap Cubes to build designs that show one half of your color and one half of your partner's color. Try to make each design different from those you have already built.

- Be ready to talk about how you made your designs.

The Bigger Picture

Thinking and Sharing

Create a display of children's work by asking volunteers to group their smallest designs together on a table. Then have children place each of the next larger designs on the table until all the designs are grouped according to the total number of Snap Cubes used.

Use prompts such as these to promote class discussion:

- What is the same about each group of designs? What is different?

- Which groups show halves in the same way? Which show halves in a different way?

- (Hold up two designs of the same colors but which have different numbers of Snap Cubes.) These two designs use different numbers of (name the color) cubes. How is it that these both show halves?

- Do you notice any pattern in the numbers of Snap Cubes used in the designs? Explain.

- Do you think that you could use seven Snap Cubes to make a design that is one half one color and one half another? Why or why not?

- How could you show halves in a design made with 20 cubes? with 50 cubes? with 100 cubes?

Drawing and Writing

1. Have children draw several designs on Snap Cube grid paper that show halves. Tell them to color the designs so that one half of each is red.

2. Have children draw a blue-and-red design that is not one-half red. Ask them to explain why one half is *not* red.

Teacher Talk

Where's the Mathematics?

The activity helps children understand that one half does not only mean one of two individual items (which is a typical understanding in young children) but, rather, one of two equal parts, whatever the size of the parts. The two parts of a figure must be equal to each other in some way if each is to show "one half." Some children will be just developing their notions of the meaning of *half*, whereas others may be able to use numerical ideas to express their understanding.

Some children will notice halves by observing patterns in their designs. Children who produce designs with patterns such as the ones below may not have to count cubes to convince themselves that the designs show halves.

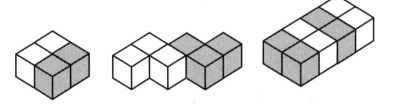

In designs in which there is no obvious pattern, children—especially the younger ones—will count to verify halves. Even for two of the same design with four cubes of one color and four cubes of another color, if the arrangement of colors within the design differs, as in the designs that follow, children will probably count to be sure each shows halves.

Extending the Activity

1. Ask children to take ten cubes of two colors and make a two-layer design made up of half of each color.

2. Challenge pairs of children to find the greatest number of ways to show halves using just four cubes.

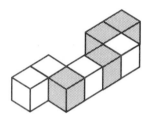 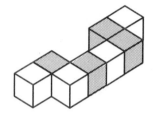

In the course of the class discussion, children may be surprised to learn, for example, that three cubes in a six-cube design and five cubes in a ten-cube design both represent one half. As they look at more examples, children can begin to understand that the amount in the half depends on the amount in the whole and that the greater the number of cubes in the whole design, the greater the number of cubes in the half. Children will be exposed to the concept of equivalency as they see one half expressed as two out of four, three out of six, four out of eight, and so forth.

If the class is large enough, it is likely that there will be at least one design for each possible roll of the die. That means that there will be designs on display with 2, 4, 6, 8, 10, and 12 Snap Cubes. Some children may observe that there is always an even number of Snap Cubes in a design, even in cases when the number rolled is odd. Although they may not be able to connect the evenness to the doubling of each roll of the die, they may be able to use the even number pattern to conclude that it would not be possible to have a design with an odd number of Snap Cubes that shows halves.

SNEAK A PEEK

- Counting
- Sampling
- Addition
- Making predictions

Getting Ready

What You'll Need

Snap Cubes, 10 in any combination of 2 colors per group

Peek boxes* to hold Snap Cubes, 1 per group

Overview

Children take turns peeking into a box and sighting one Snap Cube at a time in order to predict how many cubes of each of two colors are in the box. In this activity, children have the opportunity to:

- ◆ collect and analyze data
- ◆ use sampling to make predictions
- ◆ work with combinations of numbers whose sum is 10

The Activity

* Here's how to make a peek box: 1) Cut a facial tissue box in half. 2) Tape up the top opening. 3) Place 10 cubes in some combination of two different colors inside. (Some of the boxes may contain the same combination of colors.) Make sure that the cubes are all loose. 4) Nest the two halves of the box together and tape it shut. 5) Cut off a corner of the box so that a single Snap Cube inside the box will be visible, but will not fall out through the hole.

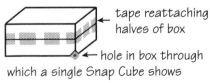

tape reattaching halves of box

hole in box through which a single Snap Cube shows

Introducing

- ◆ Place four red Snap Cubes and one black Snap Cube in an empty peek box.
- ◆ Show the peek box and tell children that there are five Snap Cubes inside and that they are to predict the colors of the cubes.
- ◆ Pass the box around the class. Have each child shake it and tilt it until a cube shows in the corner hole. Have each report the color to the class. Record the data on the chalkboard as they answer, making tallies for each of the two colors.
- ◆ After children have all had a turn, ask them to look at the data and predict what is in the box. Ask them to give their reasons. Write down their predictions.
- ◆ When children seem fairly confident of their predictions, show them the contents. Discuss how the data collected with the tally marks reflects the actual contents.

On Their Own

> **Can you predict how many Snap Cubes of each color are in a peek box?**
>
> - There are 10 cubes in your group's peek box. Have someone shake and tilt the box until a Snap Cube appears in the hole. What color is the cube?
>
> - Take turns shaking the box and recording the color that each group member sees.
>
> - Keep on sneaking peeks until you think you have enough data.
>
> - Now use your data to predict the colors and how many of each color are in your box.
>
> - Be ready to show your data to the class and report on your predictions and your reasons for making them.
>
> - Do not open the box until after you report to the class.

The Bigger Picture

Thinking and Sharing

After each group has shown its data, shared its predictions, and justified those predictions, open the group's box and show its contents.

Use prompts such as these to promote class discussions:

- How many times did each of you peek into the box?

- Would anyone make a different prediction from this data? If so, what would your prediction be?

- Look at the data from these two groups. Do you think they both have the same color combination in their boxes? Why or why not?

- Now that you have seen the contents of your box, do you think your group made a reasonable prediction? Explain.

Extending the Activity

Provide a collection of boxes and three colors of Snap Cubes for children to construct their own peek boxes. Collect class data for each one over a period of time. After they have taken a great many peeks into a particular box, call children together and have them make predictions for the contents of the box.

Where's the Mathematics?

The mathematical principle involved in this activity is called *sampling*. A statistician uses this method when interviewing a sample of the population about how people plan to vote in order to make inferences about how the entire population is likely to vote. If the sample size is too small, the results may not be an accurate indication of how the larger population will actually cast its votes. On the other hand, if the sample size gets too large, the study may become unwieldy, costly, and time-consuming without much new information being learned. Statisticians are trained to determine appropriate sample sizes for given situations.

Encourage children to pass the box around within their group several times in order to make a good-sized sampling. Groups that make a prediction after only a few samples may find that their guesses are not as accurate as those that took a great many samples. On the other hand, some children get carried away and want to make hundreds of observations. If they stop periodically and review the results, they may see that they are not gaining any new information; they are just confirming what they could have predicted earlier.

As they collect the data, children can see how tally marks, made in groups of five, can contribute to tracking their total data. They may even group the tally marks into pairs and count by tens. As they analyze the data, children will have the opportunity to develop some proportional thinking skills. For example, when they look at the data below, children may reason that there are definitely more red than black Snap Cubes in the box. They may further reason that if there were 6 red and 4 black, the tally marks would probably be closer in number than they are in this data, and so there are probably 7, 8, or 9 red in the box. Another child might counter that if there were 9 red in the box, there would only be 1 black, and these tallies don't "look" as if red came up 9 times as often as black; and so, there are probably only 7 or 8 red cubes.

⊬⊬⊬ ⊬⊬⊬ ⊬⊬⊬ ⊬⊬⊬ I ⟵ 21 Red tally marks	
⊬⊬⊬ ⟵ 5 Black tally marks	

If two or more groups are working with peek boxes that contain the same color combinations, an opportunity arises to compare the data sets. If one group has displayed the data shown above and its box contains 8 red and 2 black, and then another group displays the data shown on the next page, children may see similarities in the sets of data that may lead them to make the same prediction of 8 red and 2 black cubes.

‖‖ ‖‖ ‖‖ ‖‖ ‖‖ ‖‖ ‖‖ ⟵ 27 Red tally marks	
‖‖ ‖ ⟵ 6 Black tally marks	

Even if the other group has very different data, such as that shown below, encouraging the children to discuss how the data looks different and leads to a different prediction may be worthwhile.

‖‖ ‖‖ ‖‖ ⟵ 15 Red tally marks	
‖‖ ‖‖ ‖‖ ‖ ⟵ 16 Black tally marks	

When children are asked to compare the contents of the box to the prediction and determine whether the results are "reasonable," they begin to see that although predictions have room for error, they should still be fairly close to the actual answer. If a group took a very small sample and then predicted 8 red and 2 black and later learned that the box contained 5 red and 5 black, children may argue incorrectly that the results are close because 5 and 8 and 5 and 2 are each only three numbers apart. Other children may focus on 5 red and 5 black as equal numbers, realize that a prediction of 8 red and 2 black means many more red than black, and conclude that the prediction is not very close at all. On the other hand, if a group predicts 8 red and 2 black and the contents of the box reveal 7 red and 3 black, the prediction would have been reasonable.

Some children may think that there are more of a particular color cube in a box because they like that color. Only after many experiences with these sorts of activities will children begin to have confidence in their abilities to predict something based on observation and on information they have collected. This activity can help children recognize the varying combinations of numbers that add up to ten and gives them practice with that information.

It is important for children to have opportunities to deal with uncertainty, even with a simple and presumably "safe situation" such as these peek boxes, so that they can deal later on with statistics which could have impact on more serious issues in their lives.

SOME SUMS

- Counting
- Addition
- Making predictions

Getting Ready

What You'll Need

Snap Cubes, about 100 per group

Dice, 1 pair in 2 different colors per group

Overhead Snap Cubes (optional)

Overview

Children use Snap Cubes to keep track of the outcomes of rolling a pair of dice. In this activity, children have the opportunity to:

- reinforce number recognition
- use counting and addition skills
- collect data
- discover that certain sums on the dice are more likely to occur than others

The Activity

Introducing

- Show children a pair of dice of two different colors (for example, one red and one white).
- Have a child roll the dice.
- Ask one volunteer to build a train with the same number of Snap Cubes as the number on the red die. Ask another volunteer to build a Snap Cube train to match the number on the white die. Snap the two trains together and ask what sum the combined train represents. Set the train aside.
- Repeat rolling the dice and building trains two more times.
- Point to the three combined trains. Ask children what they think would happen if everyone in the class rolled the dice and built some trains. Would they get the same trains or different trains?

On Their Own

> ### Can you predict the sum you will roll on a pair of dice?
>
> - Work with a group. Get ready to take turns rolling a pair of dice again and again.
>
> - Each group member should predict which sum will be rolled most often. Write down your predictions.
>
> - Roll the dice. One of you makes a Snap Cube train as long as the number rolled on the white die. Another of you makes a train as long as the number rolled on the red die. Someone else snaps the 2 trains together and tells the sum.
>
> - Keep on rolling the dice and building Snap Cube trains until you have used up all the Snap Cubes.
>
> - Sort all the trains according to their lengths.
>
> - Compare the lengths of your trains to the predictions you made about the sums.
>
> - Be ready to tell how well you predicted.

The Bigger Picture

Thinking and Sharing

Call children together and discuss what they found out in their groups.

Use prompts such as these to promote class discussion:

- What predictions did you make before you first rolled the dice?

- What was the greatest sum? the least sum?

- Did some sums come up more often than others? Which ones? Why do you think this happened?

- Did you notice any other patterns? Explain.

- How many different ways could you find a sum of two? of five? of seven? of nine?

Drawing

Ask children to choose a number between 5 and 10. Tell them to pretend that their number is the sum rolled on a pair of dice. Have them draw the faces of a pair of dice that show their sum. Ask them to do this in as many different ways as they can. For example, they would show a sum of 8 by drawing the following:

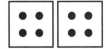 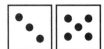 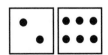 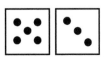 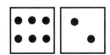

Extending the Activity

1. Have children pool all the groups' trains and see which sum(s) occurred most often in the class. Discuss how class results compare to individual group results.

Where's the Mathematics?

In addition to giving the children opportunities to work with sums between two and twelve, this activity also introduces children to the notion that when a pair of dice are rolled, sums of six, seven, and eight come up more often than others. Many children will initially predict that all the sums are equally likely, especially if three different sums occurred when you were introducing the activity. Other children are likely to predict that certain "favorite" numbers will come up most often.

Since this activity is about probability, the results that your class experiences may differ slightly from what is theoretically probable. Your class might have sums of five and seven occur most often and four and five a distant third and fourth, with eight hardly showing up at all.

When asked to explain why certain sums come up more often than others, children are likely to point out the different combinations that can form those sums. For example, there are three combinations that form a sum of seven (4 + 3, 6 + 1, and 5 + 2), but a sum of three can only be formed from one combination (1 + 2). If they used different-colored dice, some children may point out that there are actually twice as many combinations because a red four and a white three gives a sum of seven just as a red three and a white four will; so there are six ways to get a sum of seven but only two ways to get a sum of three.

If children seem interested in exploring all the combinations, you may want to tally their responses on a chart like the one on the next page.

As they examine the charted data, children might recognize that all the even sums have an odd number of combinations and all the odd sums have an even number of combinations.

Depending upon their experience with dice, some children may be puzzled initially that they cannot roll a sum of one even though there is a one on each die. Some children may have expected higher sums than twelve, so the range of two to twelve as sums may surprise some children.

2. Ask each pair of children to select a sum, such as four, and count all the Snap Cubes in the trains with a sum of four. What strategy do they use? Do they re-snap the cubes into trains of ten and count by tens? Do they count by twos? by fours?

Red Die	White Die	Sum	
1	1	2	— one way to roll 2
1	2	3	} two ways to roll 3
2	1	3	
1	3	4	
3	1	4	} three ways to roll 4
2	2	4	
1	4	5	
4	1	5	} four ways to roll 5
2	3	5	
3	2	5	
1	5	6	
5	1	6	
2	4	6	} five ways to roll 6
4	2	6	
3	3	6	
1	6	7	
6	1	7	
2	5	7	} six ways to roll 7
5	2	7	
3	4	7	
4	3	7	
2	6	8	
6	2	8	
3	5	8	} five ways to roll 8
5	3	8	
4	4	8	
3	6	9	
6	3	9	} four ways to roll 9
4	5	9	
5	4	9	
4	6	10	
6	4	10	} three ways to roll 10
5	5	10	
5	6	11	} two ways to roll 11
6	5	11	
6	6	12	— one way to roll 12

TEN TOWERS OF TEN

• Addition
• Chance
• Equations

Getting Ready

What You'll Need

Snap Cubes, 60 of each of 2 colors per pair

Die, 1 per pair

Ten Towers of Ten game board, 1 per pair, page 101

Ten Towers of Ten recording sheets 1 and 2, 1 each per pair, pages 102-103

The Activity

You may wish to have children play in teams of two rather than as individual players. This will require fewer materials and provide opportunities for children to communicate mathematically.

Overview

In this game for two players, children roll a die and choose the corresponding number of Snap Cubes in an effort to construct 10 towers of exactly 10 cubes each. In this activity, children have the opportunity to:

◆ work with the various sums of 10

◆ write simple number sentences

◆ discover the randomness of a roll of a die

Introducing

◆ Have a volunteer roll a die three times. Using one color of Snap Cubes, make three towers having numbers of cubes equal to the numbers rolled.

◆ Tell children that you want each tower to grow taller until it has exactly 10 cubes. Have another volunteer roll the die. Ask if the number rolled would help you make any of your towers into a tower of ten. Take cubes of a second color to match this roll and add them to the tower children suggest.

◆ Continue having volunteers roll the die and add to the towers, switching the colors of cubes for each roll. Explain that if a number rolled is too large for any of the towers, it is a missed turn.

◆ After all three towers are built, point out the number of rolls it took to complete each by counting the color changes. For example, if a tower has 4 yellows, 3 blues, 2 yellows, and 1 blue, the tower was completed in four rolls.

◆ Have children help you write a number sentence for each tower using the total number of each color of cube. For the tower described above, there are 6 yellow cubes and 4 blue cubes, so the number sentence would be either $6 + 4 = 10$ or $4 + 6 = 10$.

On Their Own

Play *Ten Towers of Ten!*

Here are the rules.

1. This is a game where 2 or more teams play together. Each team has 2 players. The object is to complete 10 towers of 10 Snap Cubes.

2. Each team needs a pile of Snap Cubes in 2 colors and a game board that looks like this:

3. Teams take turns rolling a die 10 times. For each number that they roll, they begin to build a tower on one square of the game board. All towers should be the same color.

4. Then, teams take turns rolling the die once. Each team uses the number it rolls to add Snap Cubes of the second color to a tower.

5. Teams keep rolling the die and adding to the towers, changing colors each time.

6. If a team rolls a number that it can't add to any tower without going over 10, that team misses a turn.

7. The game ends when all teams get 10 towers of 10.

8. Each team completes 2 recording sheets. Teams color to record each tower. Then they write a number sentence for each. For example, if a tower has 7 green cubes and 3 black cubes, the number sentence would be 7 + 3 = 10 or 3 + 7 = 10.

• Play the game again.

• Be ready to talk about how many rolls you needed to build your towers.

The Bigger Picture

Thinking and Sharing

Invite children to post their recording sheets, discuss their games, and describe some of the strategies they used to complete their towers.

Use prompts such as these to promote class discussion:

◆ What was the least number of rolls you needed to complete one tower of ten? What was the greatest number of rolls?

◆ What is the greatest number of rolls it could possibly take to complete one tower? What is the least number?

- What was your team's total number of rolls for all your towers? How much greater or less is your team's total than another team's total?

- Did you have any rolls in which you missed a turn? Why?

- Were there any strategies that helped you avoid missing turns?

- How would it change the game if you used a die with only ones and twos on it? How about a die with all fives?

Teacher Talk

Where's the Mathematics?

This game provides children with practice for working with sums of ten. Children also use number recognition as they translate the number of dots rolled on a die to the corresponding number of Snap Cubes. Finally, they use numbers greater than ten when they find the grand total of rolls. Some children may do this by adding the number of rolls for each of the ten towers. Other children may simply count the number of color changes moving from one tower to the next. Still other children may use both approaches as a check on their work.

Children will find that two is the least number of rolls needed to complete one tower. They could complete one tower in two turns by rolling 4 and 6, 5 and 5, or 6 and 4. Many children will have towers made in this way. On the other hand, it could take ten rolls to complete one tower, since in theory, a 1 could be rolled repeatedly. In practice, this is not very likely to happen, so children are apt to report that the greatest number of rolls it could take to build a tower is equal to the greatest number of color changes shown by one of their towers.

Children will be exposed to the commutative property of addition when they compare number sentences, such as 6 + 4 = 10 and 4 + 6 = 10, and towers built in the sequences 2 + 3 + 5 or 2 + 5 + 3. Children develop ease in adding short columns of numbers. This helps to dispel the idea that addition involves finding the sum of only two numbers. Some children may begin to recognize that the order in which numbers are added does not matter. This cuts the work of learning the addition facts in half!

Children apply the associative property of addition when they group the colored cubes to arrive at the number sentence that they will record. For

Extending the Activity

1. Have children play the game with a different die. For example, they can use a die with three faces marked 1 and three marked 2, or a decahedron die with faces numbered 0 through 9.

2. Have children play the game with different numbers of different-sized towers, such as five towers of twelve cubes each.

3. Have children play the game using two die—one with high numbers on it and one with low numbers. Players can choose which die they want to use for each roll.

example, for the tower below consisting of 2 yellow, 3 blue, 4 yellow, and 1 blue, like colors are grouped as (2 + 4) + (3 + 1), for which children would write the number sentence as 6 + 4 = 10.

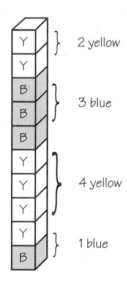

When children discuss whether they had any rolls that caused them to miss a turn, some may point out a strategy that they developed to minimize these missed turns. For example, if they had a tower of 7 and a tower of 4 and they rolled a 3, they would be better off to add the 3 cubes to the 7 tower, thereby completing one tower and leaving room on the 4 tower for any number of cubes from 1 to 6 that might be rolled next. Applying this strategy requires critical thinking, especially early in the game when children must look at many towers before they decide which tower is the best candidate for receiving the Snap Cubes.

THE DISAPPEARING TRAIN

- **Subtraction**
- **Addition**
- **Making predictions**

Getting Ready

What You'll Need

Snap Cubes, 20 per pair

Die, 1 per pair

Overhead Snap Cubes and/or Snap Cube grid paper transparency (optional)

Overview

Children roll a die to determine how many cubes to remove from a Snap Cube train. They collect data about how many rolls of the die it would take to make their train disappear. In this activity, children have an opportunity to:

- ◆ use subtraction
- ◆ collect data
- ◆ interpret a graph of collected data

The Activity

You can adapt the difficulty of the On Their Own to the level of your students by starting with 10, 15, or 30 cubes instead of 20.

Introducing

- ◆ Build and display a Snap Cube train with ten cubes.
- ◆ Call on a volunteer to take turns with you at rolling a die. After each roll, remove that number of Snap Cubes from the train. If the number rolled is greater than the number of Snap Cubes left, then roll again.
- ◆ Continue until all the Snap Cubes have been removed and the train has disappeared.
- ◆ Record each roll on a chart that looks something like this:

Roll	Number rolled	Number sentence
1st	3	$10 - 3 = 7$
2nd	5	$7 - 5 = 2$
3rd	6	$2 - 6$ (impossible)
4th	2	$2 - 2 = 0$

- ◆ Point out that number sentences help to keep track of how many cubes are left.
- ◆ Repeat the activity with another volunteer.

On Their Own

How many rolls of the die does it take to make a Snap Cube train disappear?

- With a partner, build a Snap Cube train that is 20 cubes long.
- One partner keeps rolling the die and removing exactly that number of cubes from the train until there are no cubes left.
- The other partner keeps a record of how many rolls of the die it takes to make the train disappear and writes a number sentence to show what happens after each roll. If the number rolled is greater than the number of cubes left in the train, count that roll even though you can't remove any cubes.
- Switch roles and repeat the activity several times.
- Compare your recordings. Try to predict how many rolls you would need to make your train disappear if you did the activity again.

The Bigger Picture

Thinking and Sharing

After children have completed the activity, ask pairs to share the number of rolls it took to make one of their trains disappear. Prepare a graph by first identifying columns by writing the numbers 4 to 10 across the bottom of the chalkboard. Then record each pair's response with an "X" in the appropriate column.

For example:

How Many Rolls It Took to Make the Train Disappear						
				X		
	X		X	X		
X	X	X	X	X		
X	X	X	X	X	X	X
X	X	X	X	X	X	X
4	5	6	7	8	9	10

Use prompts such as these to promote class discussion:

- What information can you learn from this graph?
- Why couldn't you make the train disappear with just three rolls?
- What do you think is the greatest number of rolls it would take to make the train disappear? Why?
- What do you think is the least number of rolls it would take to make the train disappear? Why?
- What might the number sentences look like if it took four rolls to make the train disappear?
- Why didn't anyone need 21 rolls to make his or her train disappear?

Drawing and Writing

1. Ask children to imagine that one pair started the activity by first rolling a 4 and then a 3. Have them draw a picture of what that pair's train looked like then.

2. Tell children that it took one pair six rolls to make its train disappear. Then ask children to write a number sentence that this pair might write to show how its train disappeared.

Teacher Talk

Where's the Mathematics?

This activity gives children practice with subtraction as they calculate how many cubes they have left to remove. The concrete model reinforces the symbolic number sentences that they write.

For example, in the *Introducing*:

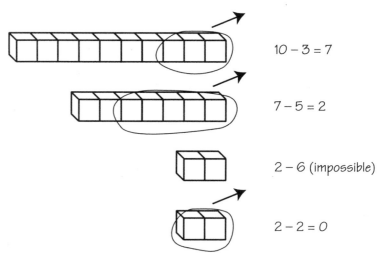

$10 - 3 = 7$

$7 - 5 = 2$

$2 - 6$ (impossible)

$2 - 2 = 0$

Looking at the Snap Cubes remaining in their trains, children predict which numbers they need to make the train disappear. Keeping a tally of the number of rolls and making a class graph will also give them practice in collecting and analyzing data from a situation that they have created.

If children have done the activity a sufficient number of times, the shape of the class graph should begin to resemble a normal curve. It will require at least four rolls of the die to make the twenty-cube train disappear because the greatest number that can occur with each roll is 6, and so the greatest number that can be rolled on three rolls is 18. Theoretically, the greatest number of rolls could be 20 if the number 1 came up each time the die was rolled. More likely, the class graph will reveal a number closer to 10 as the greatest number of rolls.

Extending the Activity

1. Have children repeat the activity starting with a train built with more than 20 Snap Cubes.

2. Have children repeat the activity, this time using a pair of dice. For each roll, they should find the sum of the numbers rolled and subtract that number of Snap Cubes from the train.

Having children figure out possible combinations of how to make the train disappear in only four rolls gives them practice in finding multiple representations for a given number. Here are some of the ways in which the train could disappear in as few as four rolls:

$$20 - 5 - 5 - 5 - 5 = 0$$
$$20 - 6 - 6 - 6 - 2 = 0$$
$$20 - 6 - 5 - 5 - 4 = 0$$
$$20 - 6 - 6 - 4 - 4 = 0$$

You may wish to have children figure this out with a train in front of them. This would enable children to pull the train apart into various configurations of four groups with no group being larger than 6, since that is the greatest possible roll of the die.

For example, for $20 - 6 - 6 - 6 - 2 = 0$:

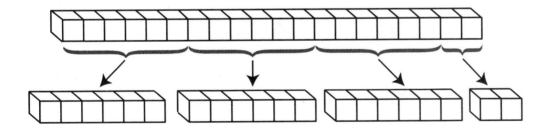

The extended versions of the activity provide practice with addition as well as subtraction. For example, with two dice, children work with the sums 2 through 12 and would need to switch to rolling just one die if there is only one cube remaining in the train.

THE HUMAN BALANCE SCALE

- Comparing
- Sorting
- Non-standard measurement

Getting Ready

What You'll Need

Snap Cubes, 50 per pair
Balance scale
String, 3 large loops

Overview

Children compare the weights of various objects to the weight of a block of 50 Snap Cubes. Then they sort the objects based on whether they weigh more, weigh less, or weigh about the same as the block of Snap Cubes. In this activity, children have the opportunity to:

- ◆ work with a balance scale
- ◆ make comparisons based on weight
- ◆ make and test hypotheses

The Activity

Introducing

- ◆ Show children a balance scale and demonstrate how it can be used to compare the weights of two small objects.
- ◆ Call for several volunteers to take turns being "human balance scales" by each holding objects such as a small box of paper clips on one outstretched palm and a box of chalk on the other outstretched palm. Ask them to close their eyes and then to think and decide which object feels heavier. Write their answers on the board.
- ◆ Ask children to predict how the real balance scale would look if the box of paper clips is heavier and how it would look if the box of chalk is heavier.
- ◆ Put the boxes on the balance scale to find the actual outcome.

On Their Own

How can you use a block of 50 Snap Cubes to weigh classroom objects?

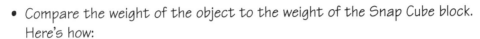

- With a partner, count out 50 Snap Cubes.

- Snap the cubes together to form a block that looks like this:

- Find a small object in the classroom.

- Compare the weight of the object to the weight of the Snap Cube block. Here's how:

    - Hold the object in the palm of one hand. Hold the Snap Cube block in the palm of the other hand.

    - Close your eyes. Decide if the object weighs *more than*, *less than*, or *about the same as* the Snap Cube block.

    - Make sure both you and your partner compare the weights. Then come to an agreement about how the weights compare.

- Find objects that fit into all of these categories:

    - *Weighs more than the Snap Cube block*

    - *Weighs less than the Snap Cube block*

    - *Weighs about the same as the Snap Cube block*

The Bigger Picture

Thinking and Sharing

Place the three loops of string on the floor in front of the room and label them *weighs more*, *weighs less*, and *weighs about the same*. Have children place their objects into the appropriate circles. Then use a balance scale and a block of 50 Snap Cubes to weigh each object. After weighing, put each object back into the circle with the label that correctly compares its weight to the block of Snap Cubes.

Use prompts such as these to promote class discussion:

- For which circle was it easiest to find objects? Why?

- For which circle was it hardest to find objects? Why?

- (Take one object from a circle.) This object came from the circle labeled ———. If it was correctly placed, how would the balance scale look with the block of Snap Cubes on one side and this object on the other?

- (Place an object and the Snap Cube block on the balance scale.) Since the balance scale looks like this, how does the weight of the object compare to the weight of the Snap Cubes?

- (Hold up the two objects that were just weighed.) Now that you have seen the weight of each of these two objects compared to the weight of the Snap Cube block, how do you think their weights would compare with each other?

You may not not have time to weigh every object that the children have found. Children will enjoy following up on this activity later during free time and using the balance scale on their own or in small groups.

Drawing and Writing

Ask children to pick an object that they know weighs more than the Snap Cube block. Have them draw a picture of what the balance scale would look like with these two objects on it. Then have them use words to describe what they drew.

Where's the Mathematics?

This activity gives children an opportunity to make conjectures about the relative weights of objects commonly found in a classroom and then test those conjectures with a balance scale. In addition, children are exposed to the concept of considering weight as one of the attributes they might use to describe an object.

A block of 50 Snap Cubes weighs just under half a pound (0.45 lb or 200 g), which fits well on the balance scales found in most primary classrooms. Also, a block of 50 cubes will fit on the outstretched palm of most primary level students.

Children are apt to report that it was easiest to find objects for the *weighs more* circle because, when pretending to be a human balance scale, it is easier to detect heavier weights. Since children do not receive much practice in discriminating among objects that weigh less than a half a pound, the ability to detect these small differences is not well developed. Nevertheless, children enjoy the challenge of this activity and the chance to get immediate feedback on the accuracy of their decisions by using the balance scale. For many children, their ability to detect the differences increases dramatically as a result of this exercise.

Children are likely to find that the hardest circle to fill was the one labeled *weighs about the same.* You are likely to see creative students bundling

Extending the Activity

1. Have children make a block of 80 Snap Cubes. Ask how they will have to rearrange the objects already in the labeled circles if they are now comparing the objects' weights to the 80-Snap-Cube block.

2. Ask children to predict how many Snap Cubes it will take to balance a pencil. Have them use the balance scale to check their predictions and compare their results with others.

3. Challenge children to suggest which combination of objects from the circle labeled *weighs less than* might exactly equal the weight of 50 Snap Cubes. Have them make some predictions and then test them on the balance scale.

---

objects such as crayons or colored markers with a rubber band in an attempt to create an object that weighs the same as 50 Snap Cubes.

Asking children to predict which way the balance scale will tip or what the tipping of the scale means will prepare them for subsequent math and science lessons in which they must add or subtract weights on the balance scale in order to determine the exact mass of an object in grams.

The question "Now that you have seen the weight of each of these two objects compared to the weight of the Snap Cube block, how do you think their weights would compare with each other?" is challenging for young children. If object A weighed less than the Snap Cube block and object B weighed more than the Snap Cube block, children will need to think critically to determine that object A should weigh less than object B. In mathematics, this is generalized in the the Transitive Property: "If $a < b$ and $b < c$, then $a < c$." This property can be applied when ordering numbers: "If 4 is less than 7 and 7 is less than 10, then 4 must be less than 10." We use the same thinking when lining up children by height, thinking, "If Alissa is shorter than Raoul and Tyler is taller than Raoul then the order of the children from shortest to tallest is Alissa, Raoul, and Tyler."

TWO-COLOR PATTERNS

- Patterns
- Counting
- Comparing

Getting Ready

What You'll Need

Snap Cubes, 80 in 2 different colors per group

Paper towel tube or rolled tube of construction paper

Pattern Stick recording sheets, 2 per group, page 104

Overhead Snap Cubes and/or Snap Cube grid paper transparency (optional)

Overview

Children create various patterns with two different colors of Snap Cubes. In this activity, children have the opportunity to:

- ◆ analyze patterns
- ◆ predict what will happen next in a pattern
- ◆ compare patterns

The Activity

Although most children will have "gotten" the pattern long before the end, children will build confidence by having their guesses supported by slowly revealing the cubes one by one.

If all children use the same two colors in the On Their Own, it will be easier for them to compare results.

Introducing

- ◆ Prepare a Snap Cube stick that is 12 cubes long and has a pattern of alternating blue and red cubes. Hide the stick in the paper towel tube.
- ◆ Show children the tube. Explain that inside the tube is a stick of Snap Cubes. Then ask them to guess what the stick looks like.
- ◆ Push the stick out of the tube so that only two cubes are showing. Ask children to guess which color will come next.
- ◆ Show the third cube and ask what color the fourth cube will be.
- ◆ Show the fourth cube. Call on volunteers to predict the color of the fifth cube and to give a reason for their prediction.
- ◆ Continue to show cubes one by one and ask for predictions about the color of the next cube until you have revealed the entire stick.
- ◆ Show how to record the stick on a *Pattern Stick* recording sheet.
- ◆ Repeat the activity with Snap Cube sticks that reflect these patterns:
  blue-red-red-blue-red-red-blue-red-red-blue-red-red
  blue-blue-red-red-blue-blue-red-red-blue-blue-red-red

On Their Own

How many different pattern sticks can you make using only 2 colors of Snap Cubes?

- With a partner, make a 2-color pattern stick that is 12 Snap Cubes long. Make sure that someone else will be able to predict your pattern by seeing only some of the cubes.

- Share your pattern with another pair. Check each other's patterns.

- Record your patterns by coloring squares on a recording sheet that looks like the one shown here.

- Keep on making and recording pattern sticks until none of you can find any different ones.

- Make sure you can describe each of your patterns.

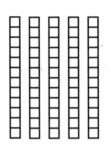

The Bigger Picture

Thinking and Sharing

Invite children to share and discuss the patterns they created. Call on volunteers to bring up their sticks and group the ones that are the same. Alternatively, you may wish to have children post their recording sheets.

Use prompts such as these to promote class discussion:

- Are any of the patterns the same? How are they the same?

- (Show two patterns that are different.) What makes these different?

- How can you tell where a pattern starts to repeat?

- Which pattern has more cubes of one color than another? How can you tell without counting?

- How can you tell what the 15th cube in any pattern would be?

- How many cubes of each color would you need to make a pattern stick twice as long as the one you like best? Explain.

You may wish to have children share their patterns by revealing them one cube at a time—as indicated in the Introducing—and having classmates predict the rest of the colors in the pattern.

Drawing

Have children draw a train of four Snap Cubes in two different colors, then lengthen the train by repeating the pattern twice more to complete a drawing of a 12-cube pattern stick.

Extending the Activity

1. Ask children to choose one of their pattern sticks and figure out how many cubes of each color they would need to make a stick three times as long; then ten times as long.

2. Tell children that they can change the pattern sticks they see into patterns they can *hear*. Lead children to agree on a "code," creating a sound for each color. For example, when they see a red cube, they might

Teacher Talk

Where's the Mathematics?

After developing many patterns and seeing them displayed, children begin to analyze patterns in terms of number and color. Younger children usually notice the alternation of color as they describe a pattern, whereas older children are more likely to attach a number to each of the colors.

The way children analyze the likenesses and differences between two pattern sticks will vary. Some children may compare a pattern stick that displays alternating green and blue cubes with another pattern stick that displays alternating red and white cubes, saying that the two sticks are different because the colors are different. Placing the sticks side by side may help children to see that although the colors are different, the patterns are the same in the way they repeat. Wherever the first stick is red, the second is green, and wherever the first is blue, the second is white.

This activity also provides an opportunity for children to see that repetition is required before a pattern is established. For example, just looking at the first two cubes does not provide enough information to predict which color will show next. Even seeing two full repeats of a pattern may not be enough to predict accurately. Some patterns can be deceiving, especially patterns that have a long repeat. A pattern like the one that follows may have children thinking that they have seen two repeats after they have seen just the first four cubes: green, blue, green, blue. Consequently, you may want to encourage children to look for three repeats of a pattern to ensure that they will not be fooled by these "tricky" patterns.

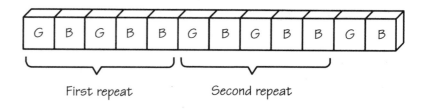

First repeat   Second repeat

clap their hands. When they see a green cube, they might slap their thighs. So, when a child holds up a pattern stick that shows the pattern red-green-green, children will interpret it as clap-slap-slap.

3. Have children imagine that they had four cubes in each of three colors. Then have them draw all the different patterns they can make with those twelve cubes.

If children can identify where a pattern begins to repeat, they can easily answer questions about which pattern stick has more of one color than another. If two pattern sticks have the same number of cubes in a repeat and the first stick has more blue cubes in the repeat than the second, then the first stick will have more blue cubes. Some children will even be able to use the number of cubes in one repeat to help them predict the color of the 15th cube in the pattern. For example, if a repeat of a pattern is red-green-green, a child may be able to figure out that the pattern ends with the 3rd, 6th, 9th, and 12th cubes, so the 15th cube will also end the pattern and will be green.

Asking children to predict the number of colors needed to make their pattern stick twice as long will require children to use proportional thinking. Many children will want to use Snap Cubes to double the length of the 12-cube pattern stick to verify their predictions.

A child who is trained to look for patterns expects to finds them. He or she expects things to "make sense." A child who sees patterns, sees the events in the day-to-day world as continuous, connected, and related. This can spill over into the area of problem solving. A child may become more persistent in trying to solve a problem because he or she expects the problem to have a solution. If the first solution is not correct, children will keep looking until they find one that works.

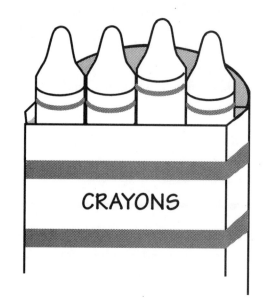

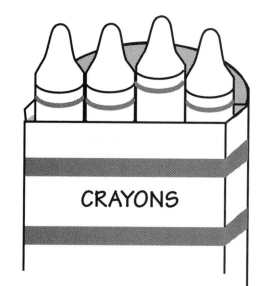

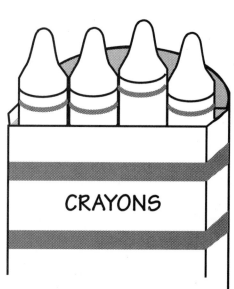

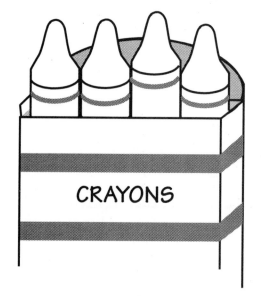

Snap™ Cubes ◆ Grades K-2

Object: _____

Estimate of length (in Snap Cubes): _____

Actual length (in Snap Cubes): _____

Our estimate was: ❏ too long
                    ❏ too short
                    ❏ just right

Object: _____

Estimate of length (in Snap Cubes): _____

Actual length (in Snap Cubes): _____

Our estimate was: ❏ too long
                    ❏ too short
                    ❏ just right

Object: _____

Estimate of length (in Snap Cubes): _____

Actual length (in Snap Cubes): _____

Our estimate was: ❏ too long
                    ❏ too short
                    ❏ just right

10	10	20	20
30	30	40	40
50	50	60	60
70	70	80	80
90	90	100	100

Record the sums: _____

How many cubes in the train? _____

How many rolls did it take? _____

- -

Record the sums: _____

How many cubes in the train? _____

How many rolls did it take? _____

- -

Record the sums: _____

How many cubes in the train? _____

How many rolls did it take? _____

- -

Record the sums: _____

How many cubes in the train? _____

How many rolls did it take? _____

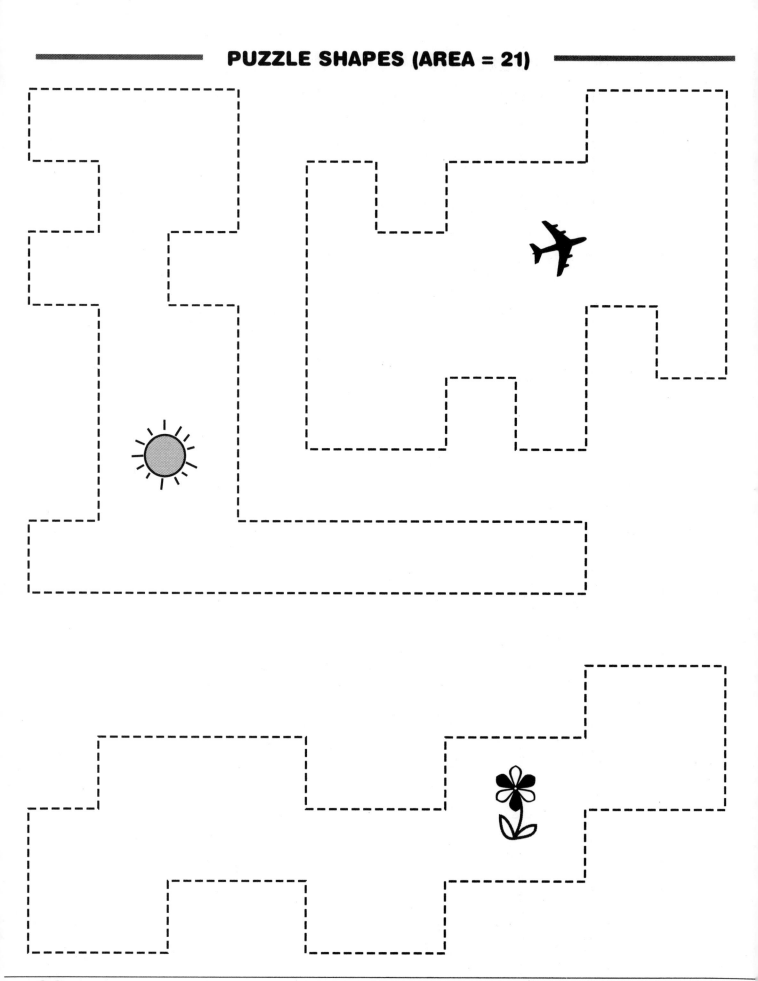

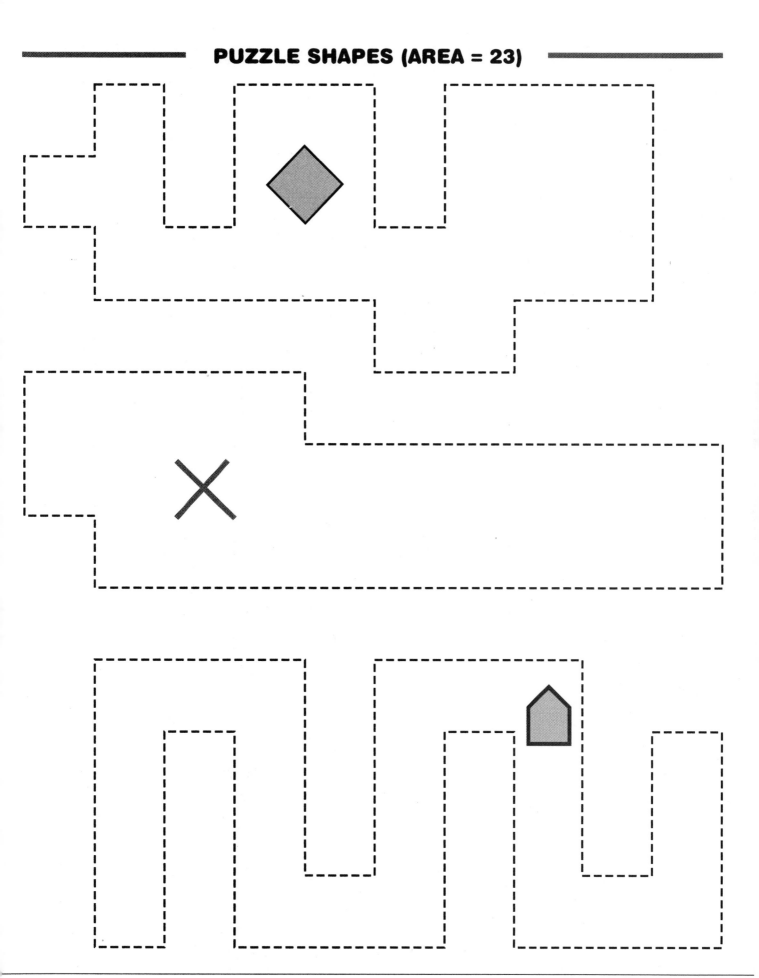

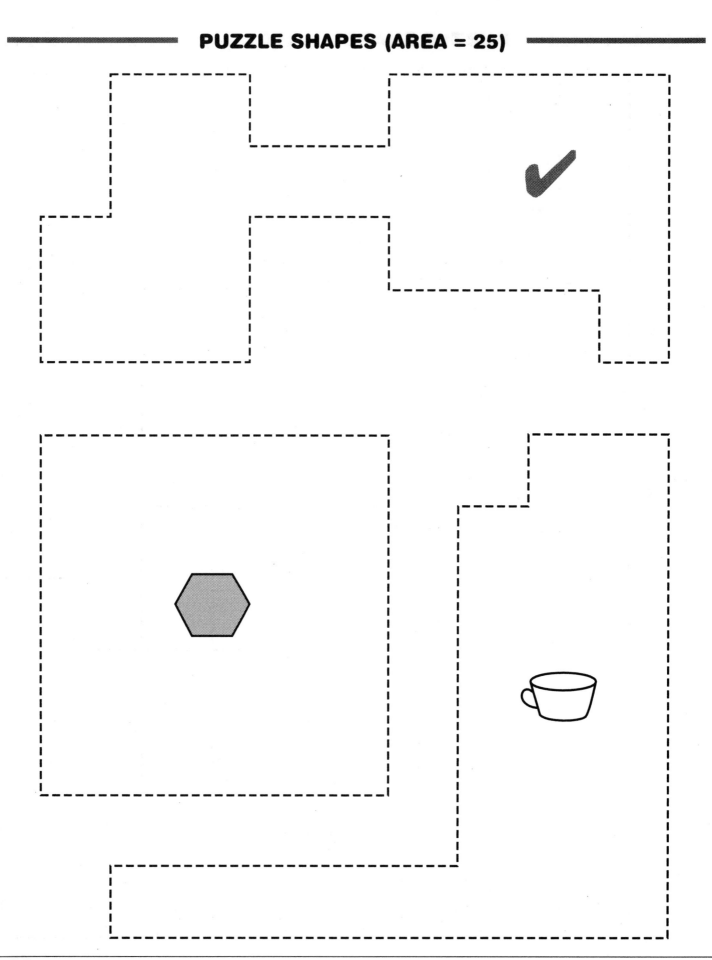

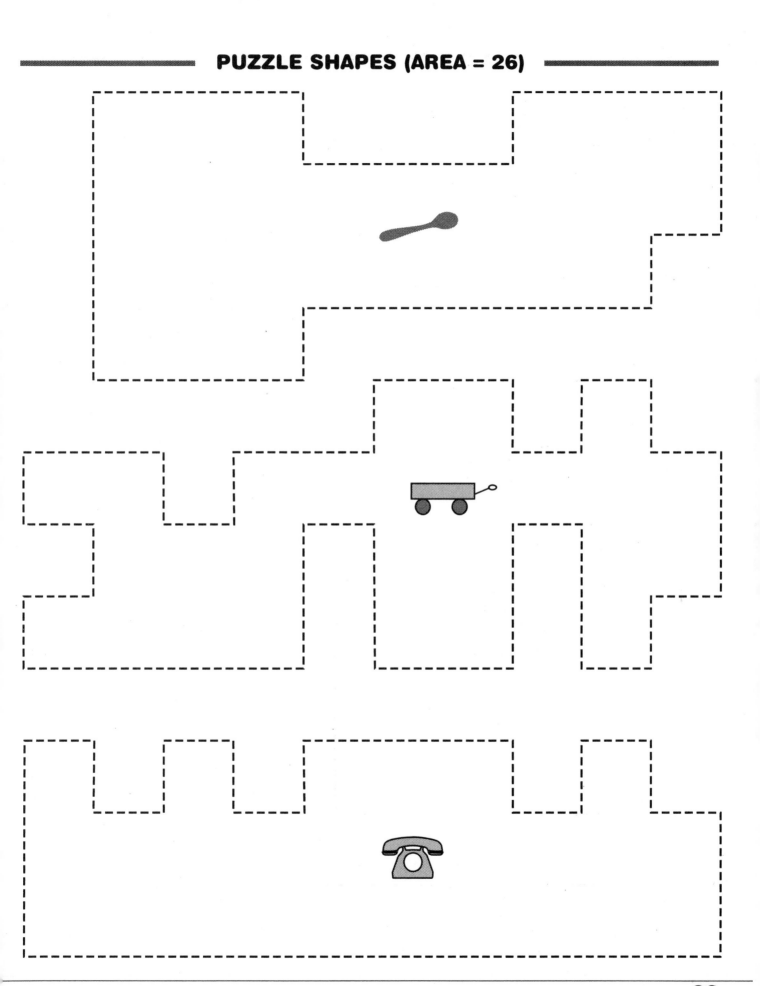

Tower 6 ☐

Tower 1 ☐

Tower 7 ☐

Tower 2 ☐

Tower 8 ☐

Tower 3 ☐

Tower 9 ☐

Tower 4 ☐

Tower 10 ☐

Tower 5 ☐

Tower 1

Number of Rolls _____

Number Sentence

___ + ___ = ___

Tower 2

Number of Rolls _____

Number Sentence

___ + ___ = ___

Tower 3

Number of Rolls _____

Number Sentence

___ + ___ = ___

Tower 4

Number of Rolls _____

Number Sentence

___ + ___ = ___

Tower 5

Number of Rolls _____

Number Sentence

___ + ___ = ___

Tower 6

Number of Rolls _____

Number Sentence

_____ + _____ = _____

Tower 7

Number of Rolls _____

Number Sentence

_____ + _____ = _____

Tower 8

Number of Rolls _____

Number Sentence

_____ + _____ = _____

Tower 9

Number of Rolls _____

Number Sentence

_____ + _____ = _____

Tower 10

Number of Rolls _____

Number Sentence

_____ + _____ = _____